Dan Lloyd's Book of Basketball

Dan Lloyd's Book of Basketball

DAN LLOYD
and
JON CULVERHOUSE

PELHAM BOOKS
LONDON

First published in Great Britain by
Pelham Books Ltd
44 Bedford Square
London WC1B 3DU
1983

© Jon Culverhouse 1983

All Rights Reserved. No part of this publication
may be reproduced, stored in a retrieval system,
or transmitted, in any form or by any means,
electronic, mechanical, photocopying, recording
or otherwise, without the permission of the
Copyright owner

British Library Cataloguing in Publication Data
Lloyd, Dan
    Dan Lloyd's book of basketball
    1. Basketball
    I. Title   II. Culverhouse, Jon
    796.32′3   GV885

ISBN 0 7207 1485 0

Printed and bound in Great Britain by
Butler & Tanner Limited, Frome and London

Contents

Acknowledgements 7
1 Story of a Star 9
2 How It All Began 22
3 The Game in Britain 27
4 Rules of the Game 39
5 England on the Move 48
6 Stars of the Eighties 54
7 Women's Scene 68
8 Coaching Skills and Tactics: Ball Handling 78
9 The Offensive Game and the Defensive Game 97
10 Better Play the Palace Way 110
11 Who Is the Greatest – Byrd or Saunders? 115
12 My Kind of Players 119
13 Stars and Stripes 126
14 Around the World 132
15 A–Z of Terms 137

APPENDICES
1 Records 142
2 Club Directory 149
Index 155

Acknowledgements

If you want to learn about a subject, write a book about it, said A. J. P. Taylor. I've learned volumes in researching and preparing *Dan Lloyd's Book of Basketball* but not before asking a lot of people a lot of questions and a lot of favours. First and foremost, I'd like to thank Dan himself for his co-operation, enthusiasm and vast knowledge and understanding of the game without which this book would not have been possible.

Roy Birch, the England women's coach, gave invaluable assistance with the women's section plus a good deal of help and advice on other aspects. Peter Sprogis and Peter Draper were always on the other end of a telephone at basketball's headquarters in Leeds, ready to talk about the game or look up some obscure statistic. I'd also like to thank Gail Davey at the National Basketball Association in New York and Charles F. Ward at the Basketball Hall of Fame in Springfield, Massachusetts, for sending scores of photographs.

Still abroad, David Turner at FIBA's headquarters in Munich kindly provided pages of statistics, while back home Richard Taylor's two painstakingly researched *Basketball Reviews* proved excellent background reading and reference books. England coach Bill Beswick was a fund of knowledge, wisdom and wit on the international scene. Mike Gibbons has supplied an excellent selection of photographs and Mike Leech, Gordon Jones and Ian Christy have provided useful additional material. Finally I'd like to thank John Pawsey for the idea, and Muriel Gascoin and Abigail Larter at Pelham for their help in getting this volume off my typewriter and on to the bookstalls.

Jon Culverhouse
September 1983

1 Story of a Star

Buried away somewhere in the files of England coach Bill Beswick is a letter from America. It arrived late in 1976 when Beswick was manager and coach of the Division Two national league side Stockport, and was from a player asking for a job. He gave details of his height (6 ft 5 ins), his weight (14 stone) and a résumé of his experience (high school and college teams in his home town of Bradford, Pennsylvania, and two years at the University of Western Carolina). Beswick, busy trying to get his fledgling league team off the ground, was always on the look-out for good Americans but this applicant didn't quite fit the bill. Beswick wrote the words 'not tall enough' across the page, put the letter in his out tray and forgot about it.

A couple of years later, when their rivals Doncaster were storming their way to the league and cup double helped at forward by a transatlantic trump called Dan Lloyd, Beswick returned to the signature at the bottom of that letter and realised that he had missed a golden opportunity.

Lloyd's tireless work for his team-mates, his high degree of skill, determination and experience, and his never-ending enthusiasm quickly made him one of the game's outstanding and most respected players. From a double-winning first season with Doncaster he moved on to Crystal Palace where he became a key member of the most successful side in British basketball history. In four seasons he collected two more league championship medals, two more cup-winners' medals and two national championship medals. Along the way he has been honoured with the captaincy of Palace and England and led the national side to a best-ever ranking of eleventh in Europe during the 1981 championships. Two other Lloyds, his brothers Dave and Doug, have followed in Dan's footsteps to make their mark on the English game.

How Lloyd came from America and ended up as captain of the England team is quite simple, and Beswick, now national coach himself, looks back with a chuckle at the irony of his oversight. For what he didn't know at the time and what Lloyd didn't tell him because he didn't appreciate its significance, was that as the son of an English emigrant Lloyd was in fact British.

Beswick had turned him down as an American because of his height: There were plenty around at nearly 7 ft. But as a British player Lloyd was a different proposition altogether. In the maze of rules which allows clubs to blend American expertise with home-grown talent, without allowing the former to swamp the latter, provision is also made for the player with a foot in both camps. These are the dual nationals who, like Lloyd, have been born or brought up abroad but are entitled to a British passport. In addition to two Americans, clubs are allowed two dual nationals to supplement their English contingent.

Players able to combine native American basketball know-how with a dual national qualification are always in demand and someone of Lloyd's ability is a rare find. It was this status which gave Dan Lloyd his passport into the English game and it is this status which has been both his driving-force and at the same time the focal point of the one show of dissent in his career.

'I've always wondered whether I would have made it in England if it hadn't been for my dual national status,' he says. 'For that reason I've always tried to play at least as well if not better than American players so people wouldn't be able to say, "Yeah, he's just here because he's a dual national." It has given me an inner drive to stay at the top of my game.'

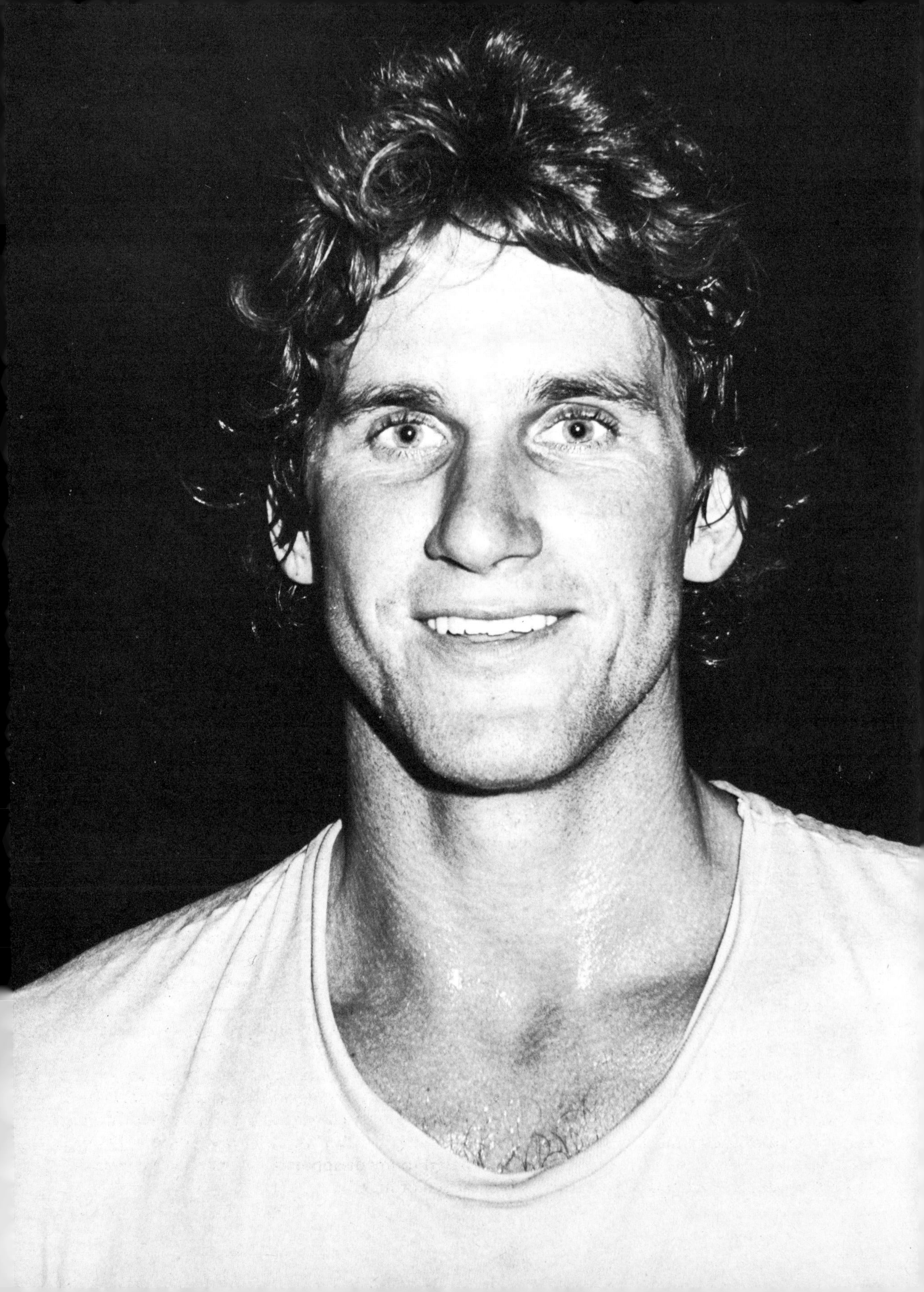

OPPOSITE: *Dan Lloyd, Crystal Palace and England*

The drive to prove himself in his chosen career has been a recurrent theme throughout his life and, as with his dual nationality, it has been the nagging doubt that perhaps he wasn't good enough which has fuelled it. First it was at high school, then at college. Throughout there was a parental voice in the background saying: 'Forget basketball, you'll never make it as a professional. Get a proper job instead.' The voice was that of his mother, charged with bringing up four young children on her own after the tragic loss of her husband, who died of a brain tumour at the age of 29. Dan Lloyd was only three at the time, hence his subsequent sketchy knowledge of his father's English background.

With a sister three years older, brothers David one year older and Doug one year younger, Lloyd grew up in a family close-knit by age and circumstances. Of necessity, early life was one of team-work and it is that quality, instilled from as far back as he can remember, which has played such an integral part in his basketball success. As American coaches are so fond of saying, there is no i in team. Lloyd was born on 13 December 1954 in Bradford, a small industrial town of about 15,000 inhabitants in the foothills of the Allegheny Mountains near Lake Erie. The nearest big city is Pittsburgh, 100 miles to the south-west. Summers are very hot but in winter the winds off the lakes bring the temperature well below zero with thick snow. 'Bradford regularly features among the nation's cold spots,' says Lloyd.

As with any small town, job prospects were limited. It was either work in the local oil refinery or get out; sport offered the one escape route to something different. For most it was only a dream but for Dan Lloyd and brothers Dave and Doug it became an achievement.

'As a kid I wanted to be a baseball star,' says Dan. 'My favourite team were the Detroit Tigers. This was back in the sixties and I used to buy baseball cards like English kids buy soccer cards. My world pretty much revolved around the game.

'We were all involved in the sport from as far

Getting to grips with American football – Dan Lloyd aged nine

back as I can remember. I played baseball because Dave played it. Whatever he did, I tended to follow. It wasn't until I was ten or eleven that I began to play basketball. None of us was particularly tall for our age: my father was about 6 ft 3 ins, my mother 5 ft 7 ins and as children we were average. It wasn't until we were about sixteen or seventeen that we really began to grow above average height.'

Basketball appealed because they didn't have a junior high school baseball team but they did have a basketball team. Playing for the school was the ultimate honour. Lloyd tried at fourteen and didn't quite make it, but the following year he squeezed in as one of the oldest members. 'I was disappointed because I thought I wouldn't have any problem but that was nothing compared to my disappointment the following year at senior high.'

Triple threat – the Lloyd brothers (from the left, Dave, Doug and Dan) dressed for winter basketball outside their home in Bradford, Pennsylvania

He'd been playing basketball all summer long, about four or five hours a day but was one of the first to be cut from the team. 'I really couldn't believe it. I'd had all these hopes and I'd worked really hard. Playing for the school, as I said, was a big thing and my pride was hurt.

'I guess it all goes back to an incident when Dave and I were walking home from practice one evening. As we went to cross the road, the school basketball coach's car pulled up at a stop sign just in front of us. As we walked in front of it, Dave just drop-bounced our ball lightly off the bonnet. Nothing big, just a drop bounce. But this guy leaped out of his car as though we'd kicked hell out of it. He was 6 ft 3 ins with a crew cut and looked really menacing. "You Lloyds, wise guys," he yelled, and he grabbed Dave's ball and fisted it way up into the air and off bouncing down the street. We just stood there scared stiff he was about to hit us. We were only fourteen and he was the last guy you'd want to wise off to. That was in the summer and it was the following term I got cut from the team!'

Instead, the local YMCA became the focal point of Lloyd's life. Dave, Doug, Dan and a couple of friends formed their own team and although it wasn't the same as playing for the school, at least they had the satisfaction of beating a few of the boys from the school team. Dan says they weren't that good as individuals but because they knew each other so well they were able to beat a lot of teams by hustling. And they really wanted to do well because there was only one court and often about 15 others waiting to play. To stay on you had to keep winning!

'I was really into basketball now. I remember during the winter, Dave, myself and Doug used to shovel snow from outside our garage so we could practise. We had a ring nailed above the door and we'd spend hours playing together even though it was freezing. Dave and I would usually end up fighting!

'The following summer I played nearly every day up in the park. I put in about eight or nine hours a day playing pick-up basketball with Dave, Doug and friends. We'd go up about noon, play until 4 o'clock, go home and have something to eat, and then go back about five and play until ten.

'That was my life, and if I didn't play it was like I'd missed something. My mother didn't like me playing so much when maybe I could have got a summer job to help the family. "You're wasting your time," she'd say. "Stop dreaming about being a basketball star and do something useful."

'But the more I played, the more I realised I wasn't getting anywhere. I didn't make the school team the following year so my friends and I decided to give basketball a miss altogether and try cross-country running instead.

'We thought, "Yeah, no one plays cross-country, we'll get in the school team that way!" We had no idea what it was all about, we just wanted to get involved in some kind of sport with the school. So suddenly this guy's got us running twelve 440s round the track and jogging a couple of miles just to warm up and we thought, "Hey, what have we got ourselves into?" We'd thought we'd mess about and get through the season.'

But it turned out to be a very demanding sport, although they stuck it out and enjoyed it, eventually becoming the top team in the district and reaching the state final. They finished last but that didn't matter!

Lloyd's first lucky break came the following summer, when he was sixteen. A return to the park for more daily eight-hour sessions of pick-up basketball coincided with a surge in growth. In the course of a year he went from 5 ft 8 ins to 6 ft 2 ins and suddenly the school team 'nearly-man' became an automatic choice.

'I was in good shape because of all my running but I hadn't played basketball seriously for two years and as far as the team went, I was a real rookie,' he says. 'I was 6 ft 2 ins and they played me guard in my first match against a couple of guys who were only 5 ft 8 ins but were ultra-quick. They were like a couple of Alton Byrds and I got about four charging fouls in the first half. It was like that for the rest of the year. We had good forwards but we were weak at guard. Other schools knew what to do, they pressed us every game!

'As the year went on, I slowly moved down the side and out of the starting five. But it didn't deter me. I still wanted to play basketball and I decided to go on to college in Bradford because I knew I could make their team. If I hadn't done that it would have meant taking a job in a factory and I knew I wasn't ready for work!'

The college set-up was relaxed and allowed Lloyd to develop his game without having a hard coach on his back. He grew to about 6 ft 4 ins and had to adjust his game: he was playing centre now and concentrated on defence. 'That was something I picked up when I first started playing and it was almost second nature. I was uneasy shooting, even from the free-throw line. I used to think I was gunning the ball! Instead I'd try to work for lay-ups or really close shots which couldn't miss.

'I spent two years at centre and it had one of the most lasting effects on my game. I concentrate now more on rebounding and defence than anything else. I'll look to shoot a bit more these days but when it comes to crunch games, I go back to playing defensively. That's the style I developed at college.'

Lloyd's next stroke of luck came in a game against New York's Jamestown Community College, ranked one of the top ten college sides in the country. They won by 40 points in New York and came to Bradford with a record of twenty-two straight wins.

'I don't know how but we managed to beat them,' says Lloyd. 'We played the whole game with our starting five because we had two players sick and two rookies we didn't dare risk. It was the most memorable win of my college career.'

It made an impression on the Jamestown coach, too, because he immediately recommended Lloyd to Western Carolina University, another of the leading college sides. 'Western Carolina had fixtures against teams like Marquette and North Carolina State, the college

30
DAN LLOYD
FRONTCOURT
6'4"   198   Senior

Bradford, Pennsylvania

Conley Comments

"Danny is an intelligent player that consistently gets the job done without as much physical talent as many of his counterparts. A team man all the way."

One of the five junior college players that transferred to WCU in '74 and contributed to last season's success... played in 20 games... considered a steady and unselfish player by the coaching staff... a heady player who executes all the fundamentals... expected to see a lot of action in key situations this winter... transferred from Pittsburgh-Bradford with a sophomore average of 16.5 points and 16.0 rebounds... played prep ball at Bradford High... plans a career in either urban planning or education.

WCU CAREER STATS

SEASON	G	FGM-FGA	.FG	FTM-FTA	.FT	Rebs.-Avg.	Pts.-Avg.
1974-75	20	18-40	.450	4-8	.500	38-1.9	40-2.0

Extract from the Western Carolina University basketball handbook 1975-76.

finalists from the year before. When they offered me a full basketball scholarship, I didn't hesitate.'

Transferring from Bradford meant that he was up against players who were already firmly established in the college team. The competition for places, the pressure-pot atmosphere of playing to packed houses of 12,000 and a far higher standard of play than anything he'd previously experienced contributed to the two most valuable playing years of Lloyd's career so far. But by the end of 1976, his final year, he had to face what he'd been trying to put off for as long as possible – getting a job.

'All the time I'd been playing basketball, I hoped I'd be able to play it professionally, and although my mother had always told me to forget the idea, it was always at the back of my mind that one day I might. But at Western Carolina I'd got as near as I could and the pro ranks were as far off as ever.'

The player who made Lloyd realise that his dream would have to go unfulfilled – in the United States at least – was his college teammate Kirby Thurston. 'Kirby was 6 ft 9 ins, 240 lb and an outstanding player. But when he didn't make even the tenth round of the draft for the pros, I knew I wouldn't either,' says Lloyd.

The next time he heard from Thurston was when a mutual friend received a letter from Germany. Kirby had got himself into some sort of trouble. 'He was a great player but he had a very short fuse,' says Lloyd. 'He wrote about a game he'd been playing out there when an opponent began yelling at him, so he hit him. The next thing he knew was that this guy's father was on court yelling at him, so Kirby hit him too. Then the guy's mother appeared. According to Kirby he would have hit her too but he got dragged away just in time!' Punch-ups apart, the letter gave Lloyd the lifeline of hope he'd been looking for. If Kirby Thurston was playing professionally in Europe, so could he.

Through his sister Kathy, who knew an American playing for Manchester, Lloyd got the addresses of some European clubs. Stockport was among those he wrote to. In the meantime, armed for the outside world with a degree in geography, he began filling in time working as a supply teacher, as a supervisor back at college in Bradford and then in a sewage plant.

The offer of a job more suited to his qualifications, as a landman with an oil company (which involved leasing land from farmers for mineral exploration), put him in a dilemma. It was a career job paying 13,000 dollars a year. If he took it there would be little chance of pursuing his basketball ambitions. But another seven days on the midnight shift at the sewage works and some more stern words from back home settled it: Lloyd set up base in West Virginia and began training with Pennzoil.

'I was still able to play basketball but not as much as I would have liked,' he says. 'The company gave me a Plymouth Fury car and I remember driving about a hundred miles some evenings just to get a game.' The European clubs he'd applied to replied saying they had no vacancies and it was another fifteen months before he got the break he so badly wanted.

With the game in England expanding, agents were on the lookout for prospective players in the United States. Lloyd filled in a form and got a call asking for more information about his father. 'Because he'd died when I was only three I didn't know a lot about him,' says Lloyd. 'There were a couple of photographs around the house of him in basketball gear so I knew he'd played in a league around Bradford, and maybe that had influenced me into taking up the game. I told the agent all I knew: that he'd been born in London and had emigrated with his parents when he was only three himself, and didn't hear any more. I still didn't realise the significance of my father being English.'

During the spring of 1978 Lloyd was kicking his heels in a hotel in Charleston, West Virginia, when he decided to call up the agent. His wife answered the phone: 'Dan Lloyd? They want you in England!'

Lloyd could hardly believe his ears. The agent was out, but another call a few hours later confirmed the news. A team called Doncaster wanted him. Then the agent told him the salary: 4,000 dollars for the season. 'By that time I'd had three raises with the oil company and I was on 18,000 dollars a year and advancing. I didn't know what to do. I badly wanted to play basketball but I had a good job and the oil company weren't going to like it if I quit.'

After talking it over with a friend, Lloyd decided to go ahead. 'I called up my boss and told him I'd be quitting soon. When I added that soon meant like a couple of days, I thought he'd be mad. But he told me it would be OK and let me leave without working out my notice.'

Lloyd made an immediate impact in his first season in English basketball. For the first time since the days of the Crystal Palace-Embassy All Stars clashes of the early seventies, there was a team to challenge Palace's supremacy.

'That season with Doncaster was in many ways my most satisfying. We had Ian Day, John Belk, myself and two other foreign players, Bryan Dunn from the United States and Cliff Bell from Canada. It was the first year of the new cup competition, which we won by beating Palace in the final, and we also won the league title. No other team apart from Palace has done that double.

'Like all other foreign players in their first season here, I wanted to do well and that helped my game. At that time I still regarded myself as American. It wasn't until towards the end of the season that I realised the significance of being dual national. As I've said already, it was a matter of pride for me not to be thought of as any less able than the other Americans in the side, so that gave me an added incentive.'

Lloyd was one of the new wave of Anglo-American imports who were to make their mark on both the domestic and international scene. His background qualified him to play for England and it was at an international training session that he met Pete Jeremich and started to hear more about Crystal Palace. Jeremich was their dual national (by coincidence, he'd been born in Bradford – Bradford, England – and had emigrated with his parents as a child) and the two became good friends.

'While I was at Doncaster all anyone ever seemed to talk about was Crystal Palace this and Crystal Palace that,' says Lloyd. 'They seemed

ABOVE: *Lloyd fends off Ovaltine's Harvey Knuckles in a league game*

OPPOSITE: *Lloyd demonstrates the perfect jump-shot action*

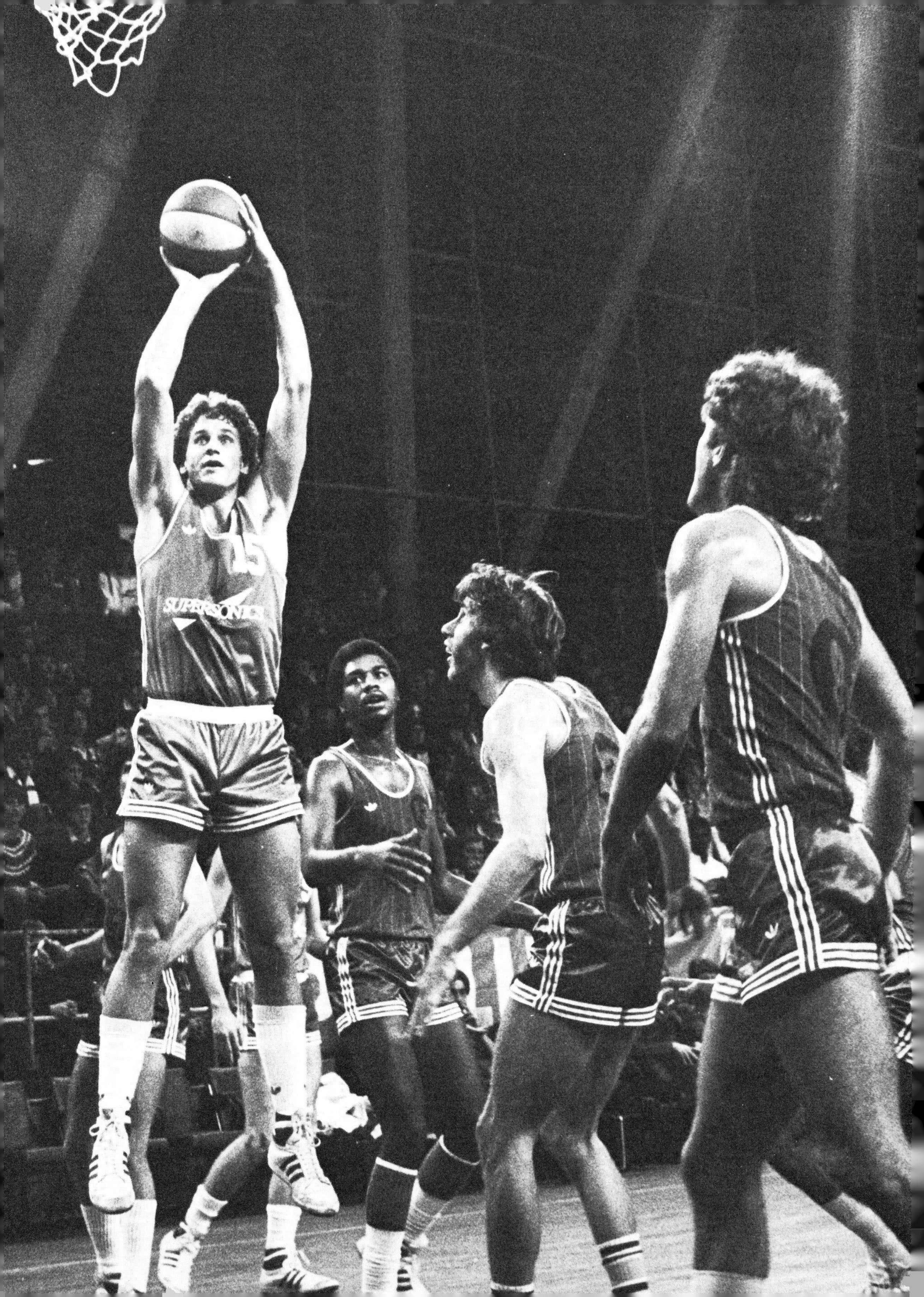
15
SUPERSONICS

to be the bad boys of the league – and they always won. We beat them in the cup and won the league that season but they won the championship at Wembley and there was always a lot of intrigue about them. I liked the idea of playing for Palace, even though I'd been very happy at Doncaster, so when they made me a good offer I jumped at it.

'At first I was a bit nervous about whether I'd be accepted down there. They had some brilliant players in people like Mark Saiers, Alan Baillie and Pete and they'd already won almost every title going.'

Lloyd needn't have worried. In his first season Palace swept the honours board. In addition to Lloyd, they had reinforced their side with a 5 ft 8 ins American dynamo called Alton Byrd and together with Baillie, Saiers, Jeremich and Englishmen Kenny Walton and Paul Stimpson, they became the first team to win the cup, league and championship treble. 'For me, that was the best side ever in the English league,' says Lloyd.

Palace went through their league season with a 100 per cent winning record and two of their defeats in an overall 45–5 win-loss record were by Real Madrid, who went on to win the European Cup. Lloyd believes that if Palace had been able to keep their squad together a European title might have been theirs, too. But with the departure of Baillie to Scottish club Murray, Saiers and Walton to newly-formed Solent and a mid-season switch of Americans, the 1980–81 season was, by Palace standards, disappointing. They won the cup, were beaten by Team Fiat for the League title and lost to Sunderland in the championship final.

While Lloyd's Palace career over the next two seasons continued to be chequered by victory and defeat in what was becoming a private championship war with Sunderland, his international career was marked by both contrast and controversy.

As England captain, he had been the mainspring of their best-ever ranking of 11th in the 1981 European championship. But his dual national status was becoming the subject of increasing rancour with him. Twice since he has been in England the rules governing dual nationals have been changed, and on each occasion Lloyd believes, with justification, that he and a handful of other Anglo-Americans have been unfairly discriminated against.

'When I first heard I qualified to play for England, I was told that that would also entitle me to register as an English player,' he says. 'In fact I joined Palace as an English player because by that time I had already played for England. Then, when it looked as though the League might be taken over by dual nationals, the English Basketball Association decided to go back to the old system and I was back where I started.

'In 1981 they changed the rules again to allow any new dual nationals to qualify as English by fulfilling a three-year residency requirement. But they didn't include dual nationals already playing here, like myself, my brother David and Pete Jeremich. We were still going to be categorised as dual nationals even though by then Pete and I had been playing in England for three years and more.'

Although Lloyd had no intention or wish to leave Palace, his future in the game would have been more secure if he were to become an English player. There was a principle, too. If he qualified to play for England, surely the domestic game should recognise him as English? In an attempt to get the rules changed, Lloyd made his protest in the spring of 1982 and hit the headlines by refusing to play for the national side. He was joined by the other two concerned, his brother David and Pete Jeremich.

A matter of a £5 daily allowance while on England duty was also at the time put forward as a reason for dissent, but Lloyd insists: 'For my part, the money wasn't the reason I refused to play. I believed that being British, playing for England and having lived in England continuously since 1978, I should have had some prospect of becoming an English player. I felt I'd served my time and given a lot to the game here.'

In most other sports Lloyd's action would have been unforgivable. But in the cosmopolitan world of basketball he received plenty of sympathy, if no response. It was the clubs who

OPPOSITE: *Coffee-time at Lloyd's London home*

STORY OF A STAR 19

The new Byrd at Palace – Dan and pet Amazon parrot Mozart

determined the rules and although Lloyd hoped his action would bring pressure to bear on them, no changes were forthcoming.

As a Palace player, Lloyd subscribes to his club's belief that there is a conspiracy to try to break their domination of the game, and it is issues like the one involving dual nationality which feed their suspicion. Whether they are fact or fantasy, Lloyd's suggestion of an independent rule-making body merits serious consideration.

Lloyd came back into the England fold in 1983, but he was no longer captain and his objective seemed as elusive as ever. 'I still believe my case is a just one but playing for England again is more important to me. I've always enjoyed the experience and I missed it in 1982,' he said. Then later in the year came the breakthrough in his campaign for recognition as an English player. From the 1984–85 season, it was planned to allow long-serving dual nationals to transfer to English registration. It had been a long battle, but worth it.

At twenty-nine-years-old, bachelor Lloyd now looks on England as his home. Most of his free time is spent with his new venture, a basketball training centre at Crystal Palace. Anticipating the rise in the game's popularity in England, Lloyd asked for and was given the job of coaching the increasing number of children and adults in South London wanting to take up basketball. The school is funded jointly by the Sports Council and the GLC with Lloyd as Director. The response has been very encouraging: in its first year the school was attracting nearly one hundred men, women and children every week.

Basketball standards have increased tremendously in recent years and the turn-out for the school convinces Lloyd that the momentum can be sustained. 'I think the American influence has been partly responsible for better standards in

English basketball,' he says. 'Better coaching and the arrival of regular television coverage have also made a big difference.

'I get kids trying things I'm certain older generation English players would never have attempted in their younger days simply because they wouldn't have known how. I believe English players have a natural physical aggression which is a vital ingredient of the game today. The main weakness is in ball handling. That's a skill which can be picked up only by hours of practice. From a practical point of view, that has to be the No. 1 priority of any player learning the game.'

Looking back on his own career, Lloyd says: 'Basketball has not only been the biggest influence on my life, it has been the biggest part of my life. It's something I always wanted to do and, despite the misgivings of my mother back home, I fulfilled my ambition. I enjoy the game because it's so demanding, physically and in terms of skill and agility. It's also a sport which requires a high level of discipline but at the same time offers plenty of scope for creativity. There are right ways of doing things but as players like Alton Byrd and Russ Saunders have shown in the English game, they can be done with flair.

'If there is a single attitude I'd like to instil in younger players today, it's the desire to do your best. It hurts me when I see players with a lot more natural talent than I have who aren't prepared to work harder at their game. So if I can convince people about just that aspect, I'll be happy.'

2 How It All Began

Romantic origins of basketball include a sport played by the Aztecs of sixteenth-century Mexico in which the participants were required to throw a solid rubber ball through a stone ring. The winner, so the story goes, was entitled to the clothes of all the spectators.

Dr James Naismith would have got a cool response had he come up with that idea while working on a new game in the United States in 1891. It was a winter of zero temperatures in Massachusetts and PE instructor Naismith, a Canadian, faced the problem of how best to dissipate the energies of students at the School for Christian Workers at Springfield (later Springfield College) where they had become fed up with the regimented rigours of gymnastics.

Naismith wanted a team game which could be played indoors, gave equal opportunity to each player and placed a premium on skill rather than strength. He chose a soccer ball for its ease of control and even bounce, ruled for reasons of space that the game should be played with hands not feet, and to place the emphasis on skill, devised a goal in the horizontal plane and out of the players' reach. To eliminate physical contact, he also ruled out running with the ball.

In January of 1892 Naismith put his idea to the test. Two peach baskets were nailed on the balconies at opposite ends of the gymnasium and he invited two teams of nine players to try to outscore each other by aiming shots into their opponents' basket.

The scoreline was only 1–0, but the result was an instant success. Naismith had formulated only a rough set of thirteen rules but he was soon receiving dozens of requests for them. By the end of the year the game had already spread as far afield as Mexico and by 1897 a national college championship was under way. The first professional league was formed in the United States two years later. Naismith hadn't just refined or adapted an existing game; he had invented a completely new one and it was called basket ball.

In the early days the ball had to be retrieved from the basket with a step ladder. Then someone came up with the idea of knocking the bottoms out of the peach baskets and the ring and net of today soon followed. Although Naismith had envisaged that the game could be played by any number up to forty players, by 1897 the five-a-side norm had been established.

OPPOSITE: *Dr James Naismith, the inventor of basketball*

BELOW: *Game and equipment in the 1890s*

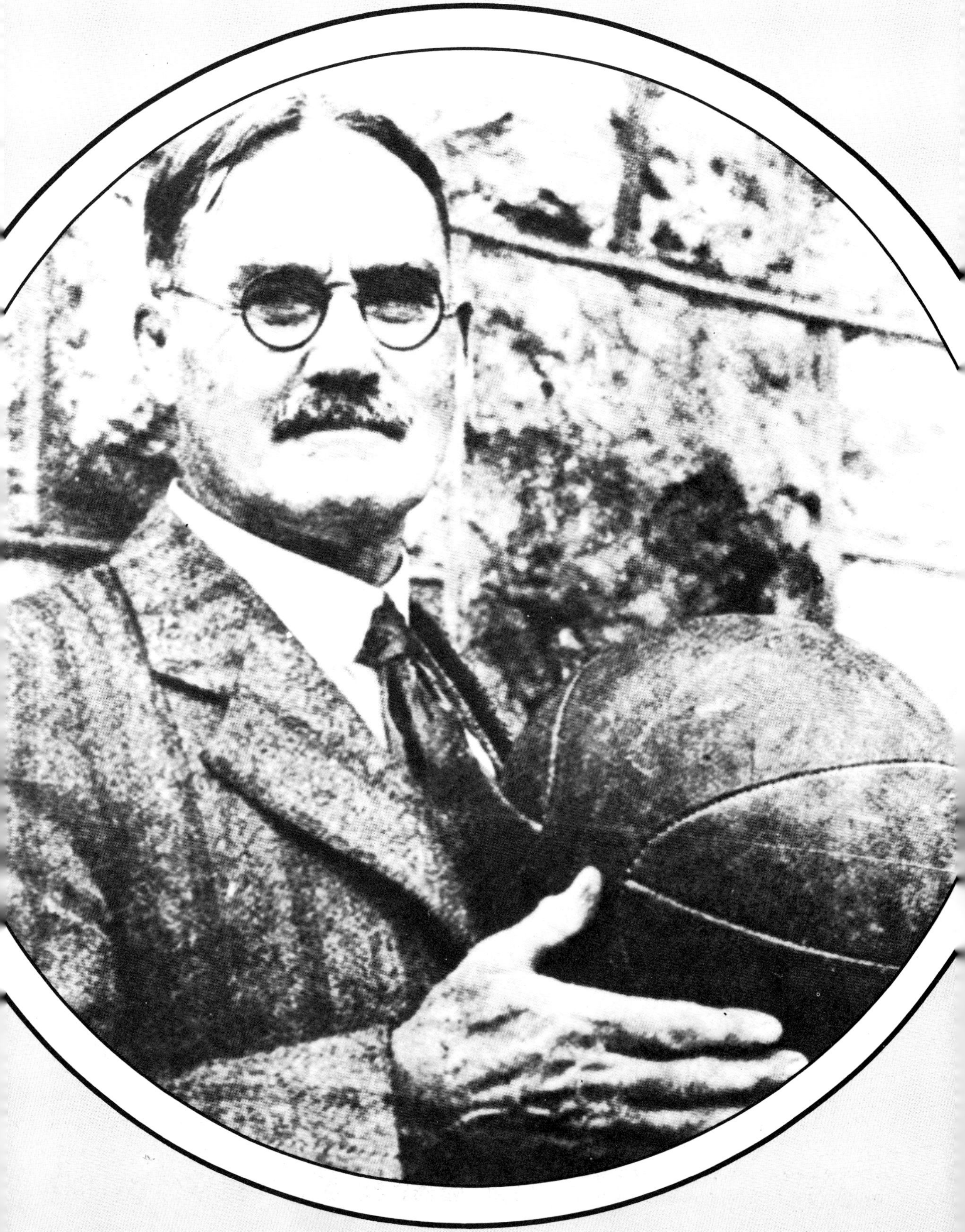

ABOVE: *The cage at Paterson, New Jersey, site of American league basketball 1919-33*

BELOW: *A drawing of the first game of basketball which appeared in the Springfield College magazine* Triangle *on 15 January 1892*

Naismith's Original 13 Rules

1. The ball, an ordinary Association football, may be thrown in any direction with one or both hands.
2. The ball may be batted in any direction with one or both hands, but never with the fist.
3. A player cannot run with the ball. The player must throw it from the spot on which he catches it, allowance to be made for a man running at good speed.
4. The ball must be held in or between the hands. The arms or body must not be used for holding it.
5. No shouldering, holding, pushing, striking or tripping in any way of an opponent. The first infringement of this rule by any person shall count as a foul; the second shall disqualify him until the next goal is made or, if there was evident intent to injure the person, for the whole of the game. No substitution shall be allowed.
6. A foul is striking at the ball with the fist, violations of Rules 3 and 4 and such as described in Rule 5.
7. If either side make three consecutive fouls it shall count as a goal for the opponents (consecutive means without the opponents in the meantime making a foul).
8. A goal shall be made when the ball is thrown or batted from the ground into the basket and stays there, providing those defending the goal do not touch or disturb the goal. If the ball rests on the edge and the opponents move the basket, it shall count as a goal.
9. When the ball goes out of bounds, it shall be thrown into the field and played by the first person touching it. In case of dispute the umpire shall throw it straight into the field. The thrower-in is allowed five seconds. If he holds it longer, it shall go to the opponent. If any side persists in delaying the game, the umpire shall call a foul on them.
10. The umpire shall be judge of the men and shall note the fouls and notify the referee when three consecutive fouls have been made. He shall have the power to disqualify men according to Rule 5.
11. The referee shall be the judge of the ball and decide when it is in play in bounds, to which side it belongs, and shall keep the time. He shall decide when a goal has been made and keep account of the goals with any other duties that are usually performed by a referee.
12. The time shall be two 15-minute halves with five minutes' rest between.
13. The side making the most goals in that time shall be declared the winners.

Various innovations followed that Naismith hadn't thought of in his original thirteen rules, including the dribble and the introduction of a backboard. This latter was to prevent spectators interfering with play from the balconies where they had a habit of grabbing shots intended for the basket. With the advent of the rebound, backboards became an integral part of the game.

There were 200 spectators at the first public match in 1892, and soon the numbers grew to such an extent that games were frequently interrupted by people encroaching on the court. The problem became so acute that the game was played inside net cages; these were eventually abandoned in 1929 but sportswriters continued to call players 'cagers' for many years afterwards.

3 The Game in Britain

Tuesday 19 January 1982 was probably the biggest day in English basketball history. It wasn't an event on court that captured the headlines but an announcement by the game's governing body.

For the first time in this country, basketball was to receive live television coverage of a weekly league game. If the immediate benefits could be counted in terms of higher attendances and hugely increased sponsorship, Peter Sprogis, former Development Officer of the English Basketball Association and the man who did more than any other to bring about basketball's 'industrial revolution', puts the longer-term benefits this way:

'For any sport to develop, it must have at its highest level a competition which attracts regular media coverage, specifically television. Basketball has had that competition, in the form of a national league, for only 11 years and until 1982 never received the type of media coverage needed to create a wider public awareness of the game. For the first time, young people can watch good players on television and copy what they do. And that is a fundamental necessity for any player wanting to improve his game. Until now basketball has not been able to provide that opportunity.'

Thus until the advent of Channel 4's Monday-night league coverage in the autumn of 1982, basketball in England had been more about tomorrows than yesterdays. Leagues had come and gone, club and international sides were making only slow progress against superior foreign opposition and, although the national league had been expanding since its formation in 1972, the recession was threatening several leading clubs with extinction.

The benefits to basketball in its first television season included an increase in league sponsorship from £50,000 to £250,000, and attendances up by 20 per cent to a record 250,000 in the First Division. On three occasions Birmingham attracted 3,000 full houses to games at the Aston Villa sports centre, the cup final was a 2,500 sell-out at Leicester and the national championships were watched by 9,000 on two successive nights at Wembley plus a television audience of 1.5 million for the final.

Perhaps it was no coincidence either that that same season saw Crystal Palace become the first British side to beat seven-times European Cup-winners Real Madrid and take the 1981 winners Maccabi Tel Aviv to the buzzer in the Philips International Tournament. Palace have been ploughing their own furrow as Britain's leading

Channel 4 arrives

ABOVE: *Ovaltine introduce their cheer leaders, the Rebel Rousers*

OPPOSITE: *Crystal Palace coach Danny Palmer after the win over Real Madrid*

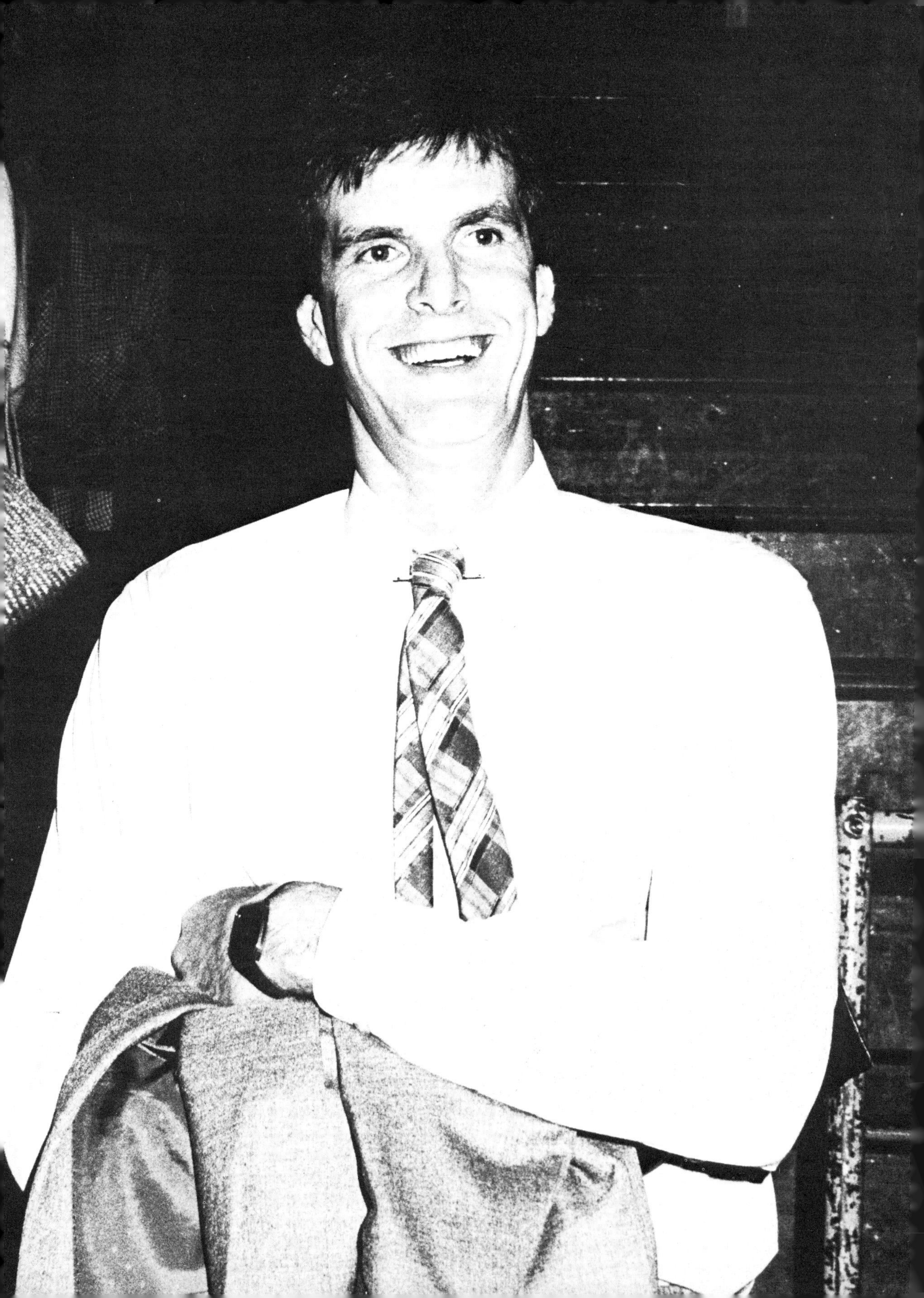

club since their formation as Sutton in 1972. In 1975 they reached the quarter-finals of the European Cup-winners' Cup and reached the same stage in 1981. The arrival of regular television coverage and increased sponsorship at a time when their own economic fortunes, along with those of many other clubs, were at a low ebb undoubtedly renewed the impetus for their historic win.

In Scotland leading side Murray (Edinburgh), inspired by Alton Byrd, have been building a team capable of challenging the best in Europe.

Internationally, England ranked only twenty-first in Europe in 1983 although the pattern of previous performances suggests our stock is rising. In 1981 England achieved a best-ever ranking of eleventh to provide a gratifying finale to ten years of hard work by their coach, Vic Ambler. The following year that progress was undermined by factors such as the absence of several leading players. But as England's new coach, Bill Beswick, points out in Chapter 5, the 1982 performance wasn't representative of the strides made under Ambler.

So there are signs that basketball is on the move in England, both on the domestic and international front. But why has it taken so long when countries like Italy, Spain and those behind the Iron Curtain have long been established as powerful forces at club and international level, not just in Europe but in the world?

It's not as if basketball was late arriving in Britain. The year basketball became an Olympic sport, at Berlin in 1936, was also the year the Amateur Basket Ball Association was founded in this country (the ABBA uses basketball as two words to avoid confusion with the ABA, the Amateur Boxing Association). The same year also saw the inception of England's first national championship.

Peter Sprogis believes the game was slow to take root partly because as a sports-oriented nation, there were too many other well-established traditional games such as soccer, rugby and cricket. Also, those who did play basketball lacked the will or the capital to organise themselves into a national league. 'We've had only 11 years of solid league competition on which to build, while countries like Italy have leagues which go back to the 1930s,' says Sprogis. 'We started out 30 years behind but I'd say we've already closed the gap to about five or six.' Although the English league is professional, it is manned almost entirely by part-time players – except for the American contingent. Leading Continental clubs have far higher proportions of full-time players.

The first attempt at forming an English basketball league was in 1939 when four London ice rink managers staged games to try to keep spectators coming back in between hockey matches. The teams comprised mainly American and Canadian ice hockey players and the 'league' lasted only a few months. It wasn't until 1960 that another league was formed. This time it was a genuine league but, without any London representation, it lacked credibility. The two most powerful London sides, London Polytechnic and Central YMCA, who had dominated the annual open championship over the previous decade (London Poly also having been runners-up to Hoylake YMCA in the first championship in 1936), felt they already had all the top-class opposition they needed. It was this kind of self-interest which, Sprogis believes, hindered the development of the game. The league grew from nine clubs to 16, including two from Scotland and one from Wales, and continued on a regional basis until 1972 and the formation of the present English national league. Before 1972 basketball was an amateur game in the true sense of the word. It was played mainly by students and United States servicemen who comprised the various YMCAs, universities and colleges that dominated the championship over the years.

The new league changed all that: 1972 ushered in the era of the professional club. The students' days were numbered because sponsorship enabled clubs to start hiring the best players. From its original six members, the league has expanded to more than 80 and includes two men's divisions, two women's divisions and a junior division.

Sprogis, who was founder-member of the championship-winning side Embassy All Stars until its break-up in 1978, believes climate is also an important factor in the rapid establishment of basketball in countries like Spain and Italy.

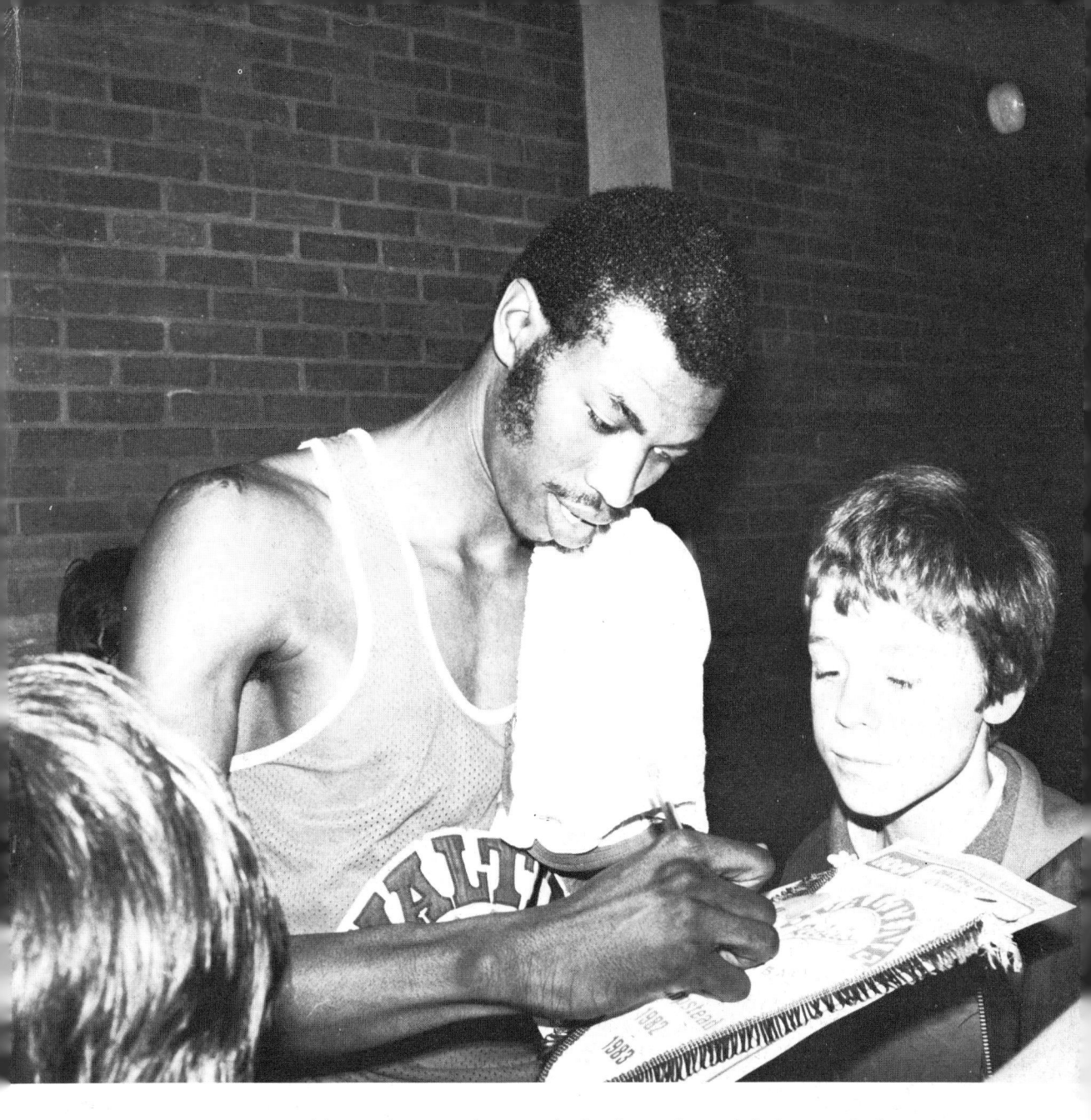

Ovaltine star Harvey Knuckles with young basketball fans

There it can be practised outside almost all year round, so it was immediately attractive as a game children could play from an early age. Here established summer games such as cricket take up many young people's time in the outdoor season.

Other early restrictions on basketball in England, says Sprogis, included a lack of facilities, a lack of people qualified to teach the game and a lack of awareness, particularly in schools. In 1969 there were only some 50 sports halls in England. Today there are 600, many with a seating capacity of more than 1,000. New ones, in North London, Liverpool and Kettering, with seating capacities of around 4,000 are planned. While these would help meet the demands of swelling attendances and children queuing to play the game, Sprogis admits that a lack of qualified coaches is the next threat to the grassroots expansion of the game. But if the demand is there, fuelled by media coverage of the national league, he believes schools and colleges will have to respond. The past lack of coaches was perhaps due more to lack of demand than lack of training facilities.

One of basketball's perennial problems has been the nationality question. Almost since the game's introduction to this country, foreign players have been a major influence. The 1938 championship final was won by the all-American Latter Day Saints, of Catford, who went on to play as 'England' in the first-ever international match, against Germany (and won 40–35). Post-war basketball was also dominated by overseas players, with the Polish Carpathians and the Latter Day Saints dominating the championship.

This led to a restriction on foreign players in the form of two championships, one open and one closed. But the problem surfaced again with the emergence of university teams boasting strong overseas content. The 1965 championship final saw Oxford University include nine Americans against Aldershot with none. On that occasion the Americans lost, but to obviate the problem, the new national league of 1972 placed a restriction of two foreign players per team. To accommodate the in-betweens, a dual national status (later ambiguously altered to 'British') was created. Teams were limited to two foreign players (almost always Americans because they were the best) and two 'British' players each. So, if teams could afford it, they could have virtually four Americans in their starting five.

Peter Sprogis has no doubt as to the value of Americans in the English game:

'I've never met any English player who has said that playing alongside or against Americans hasn't helped his game. In my opinion, Americans are the main reason for the improvement in the standard of English basketball. But success in raising the level of play has given us a dilemma. We have to strike a balance between encouraging the development of English players while maintaining standards with the contribution Americans can make. But who's to say who is English and who isn't?

'Pete Jeremich, one of the outstanding players in the game, was born in Bradford, England, but brought up in the United States. There are several more like him who want to play here. But if they play as Englishmen they're depriving English-born-and-bred players of a place in a team; and if they are made to play as Americans, is basketball being fair to them?'

The most recent example of the dual-national muddle involved John Johnson. Born in England but raised in the United States, Johnson chose to forgo playing league basketball for three years in order to fulfil a residency qualification which would entitle him to play as an Englishman from the middle of 1984. Paradoxically, Johnson is already recognised by the international federation (FIBA) as English and has thus been allowed to play not only for the national side but also in Crystal Palace's European matches. He could have played domestic basketball straight away as a dual national or American, but under the rules current at the time would not have then been able to qualify as English. Like Lloyd and co, it would have been Catch 22. However, the new rules planned for the 1984–85 season will change that situation and enable him to play now as a dual national and still qualify as English.

THE GLITTERING PRIZES

The national championships, the cup and the league, these are the three principal prizes in English basketball. And if it sounds confusing to have league champions who aren't always national champions and vice versa, the following explanation will help sort out the difference between the various competitions.

The national championship is the oldest and most prestigious competition in basketball. It started in 1936 as an open, knock-out contest and continued right through to 1978 when basketball's growth and popularity prompted a big change in the structure of its competitions. The national championship became a closed contest for the four teams who finished top of the national league. The idea was to provide a climax to the end of the season like, for example, soccer's FA Cup Final. The national championship

OPPOSITE: *Vince Brookins in action for Sunderland during the 1981-82 season*

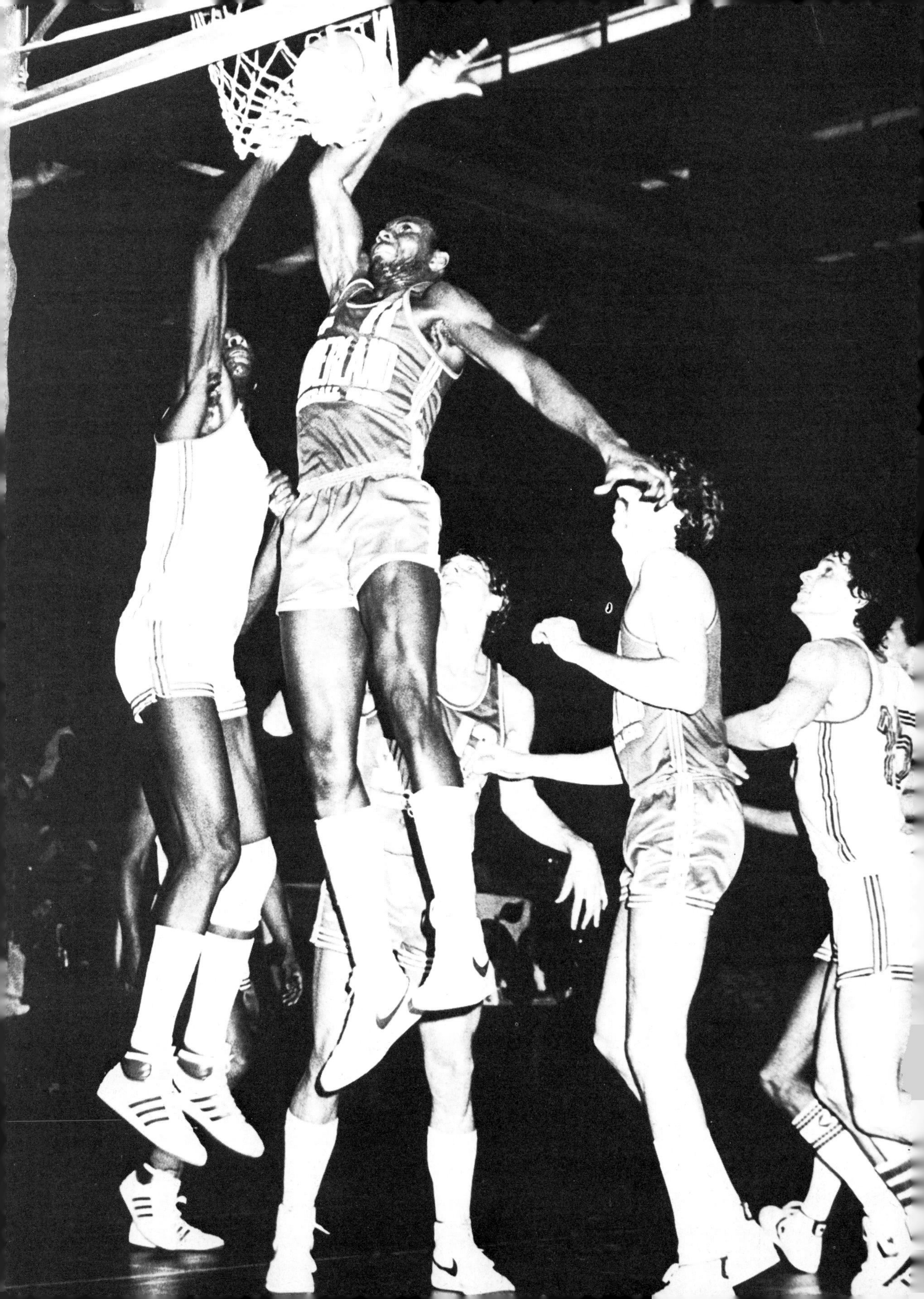

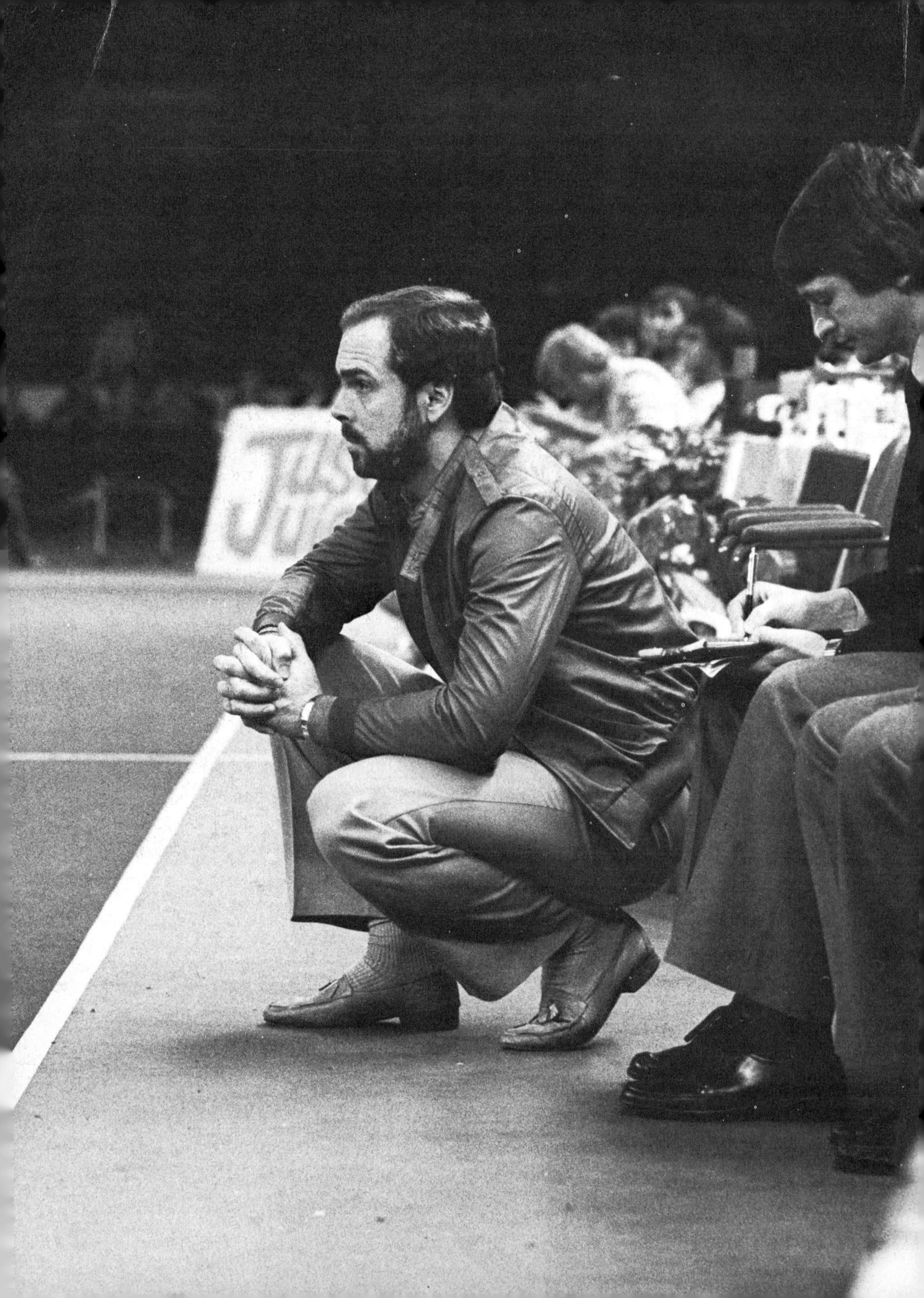

OPPOSITE: *Former Solent and England coach Tom Wisman*

ABOVE: *Basketball in action at Hemel Hempstead*

is played every March at Wembley and follows American lines with a play-off between the top four teams. The prize is the same cup, donated by George Williams, great-grandson of the founder of the YMCA, which was first contested in 1936.

To give every team, league and non-league alike a competition along the knock-out lines of the old championship, a new cup competition was introduced in 1979. Since 1981 this has been sponsored by store group Asda and carries a place in the European Cup-winners' Cup for the winners.

Last, and arguably most importantly, there is the league title. In the past virtue has been its own reward for the side finishing top of the First Division. But from 1983-84, due recognition is being given to the achievements of the league champions by awarding them a place in Europe's premier competition, the European Cup. Until 1983, this honour had always gone to the national champions.

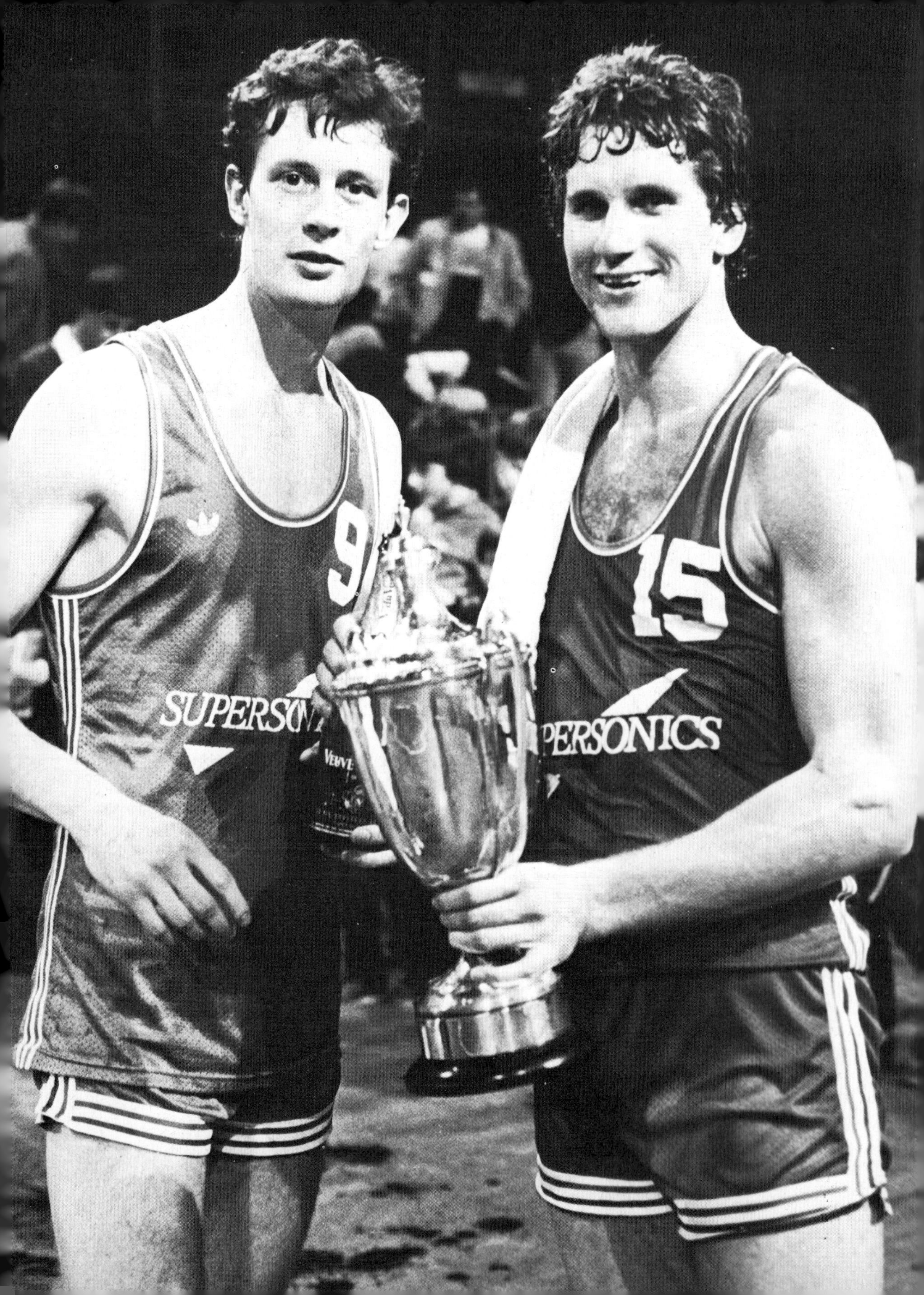
9
SUPERSON
15
PERSONICS

OPPOSITE: *We won the Cup – Dan Lloyd and Mick Bett with Crystal Palace's 1983 league title trophy*

ABOVE: *The face of defeat. Crystal Palace after losing the 1982–83 Philips Tournament to Maccabi*

Only Crystal Palace, in 1980, have succeeded in winning the treble.

Another competition which has established itself as a major attraction is the annual Philips tournament held every New Year at Crystal Palace. Here leading British clubs test their skills against some of the top clubs from Europe and North and South America.

HIGHLIGHTS OF THE NBL

1972-73 A new English league is formed with six members: Avenue (London) (who win the title), Bruno Roughcutters (Liverpool), Sutton, Loughborough All Stars, Sheffield YMCA and RAF Fliers. Non-league London Latvians, led by the first star of basketball, Peter Sprogis, defeat Sutton for the championship.

1973-74 Latvians enter the league as Embassy All Stars while Sutton strengthen their squad with two other names destined to become star turns, Jimmie Guymon and Tom Wisman, and win the league and the championship.

1974-75 Embassy-Sutton rivalry grows with the All Stars recruiting 6 ft 11 ins Steve Schmitt, who plays in a pigtail. Sutton (now Sutton and Crystal Palace) fall to league newcomers St Luke's, Exeter and Embassy, who win their own double.

1975-76 The expanding league includes two men's divisions and a women's division. SCP add 6 ft 8 ins Mark Saiers to the bench and avenge their previous season's defeats by winning back the league and championship.

1976-77 Now sponsored by Cinzano, SCP maintain the upper hand by again winning the double, while Embassy are pushed into third place in the league by ATS Manchester. There are now 36 teams in the NBL.

1977-78 Another double for Cinzano SCP but

there is anger and acrimony in the new-style Wembley championships. Embassy are beaten by a controversial on-the-buzzer basket in one semi-final against Team Fiat, Coventry, while Cinzano coach Wisman is fined and banned for smashing a chair in the final.

1978–79 Cinzano's three-year league reign is ended by Doncaster. It's the double, too, for Doncaster as they beat the Londoners (now plain Crystal Palace) in the new cup competition. At Wembley, where it's the first year of a new-style play-off between the league's top finishers, Palace beat Team Fiat in a final as tame as the previous year's was bad-tempered.

1979–80 Palace import the most exciting player seen in the English game. He's 5 ft 8 ins Alton Byrd, who helps them land the first treble. They beat Doncaster in the cup, take the league title with a 100 per cent record, and complete a hat-trick of wins over Team Fiat in the championship final. Byrd is voted the league's Most Valuable Player.

1980–81 The era of the businessman opens with Harry Smith introducing star-studded Solent to the Second Division. But a quiet American coach called Tom Becker steals the show. Cup-winners Palace lose their league title to Team Fiat and Becker's Sunderland underdogs become Wembley top dogs by beating the London club in the championship final. Byrd is again voted MVP.

1981–82 Solent win their first major trophy by beating Doncaster in the cup final by a record margin. But Palace shade them for the league title and avenge their previous year's Wembley defeat by regaining the championship title from Sunderland: their seventh championship in ten years.

1982–83 Palace lose Byrd to Scottish champions Murray but emerge from a shaky start to the season to record a historic win over Spanish champions Real Madrid in the first leg of a European Cup match. Live television coverage of league matches opens with Palace beating Birmingham in overtime watched by 3,000 fans and a TV audience of 1.5 million. Solent retain the cup and Sunderland regain the championship in a thrilling overtime finish in the third consecutive final between themselves and Palace.

4 Rules of the Game

SUMMARY OF THE RULES

If you watch basketball on television or follow your favourite team, the following summary of the rules together with a few explanations may help answer aspects of the game which aren't immediately clear. If you want to start playing basketball, or you play already, and want some more details about court size, kit and the game itself, a more comprehensive guide follows.

Scoring

Two points for a basket (field goal) during play. One point for a basket from the free-throw line following a foul.

Time

Two halves of 20 minutes with the clock stopped every time a referee blows his whistle. The clock does not start again until the ball touches a player on court.

Teams

Each team is allowed five players on court at any time, with up to five substitutes who can be sent on as often as the coach wants.

Fouls

Holding, pushing, charging or tripping players is penalised. If the incident occurs when a player is in the course of shooting, it is penalised by free throws from the foul line: three attempts to score two points. Players may commit up to five fouls after which they are disqualified. Substitutes may take their place.

Teams may commit up to a total of eight fouls in each half before each subsequent offence is penalised by two free throws for the opposition.

If a player commits three or four fouls early in the game, notice how the coach will rest him until later in the game so as not to risk having him sent off altogether.

Violations

All other offences, such as running with the ball or kicking it, are called violations and are penalised by loss of possession. Some violations involve time factors. For example, a shot must be attempted within 30 seconds of a side gaining possession; no offensive player, with or without the ball, may remain in the key-shaped area under the opposition's basket for more than three seconds; once a team has gained possession in its own half, it must advance the ball over the halfway line within ten seconds.

Why all these rules? Most have been introduced to speed up the game and make it more entertaining. The 30- and 10-second rules are to prevent time-wasting and defensive play; the three-second rule is to prevent 'basket hanging' by big players just waiting to make an easy score.

Ball

The ball is spherical, made of leather, rubber or a synthetic material such as nylon. It measures 30 inches in circumference and weighs approximately 22 ounces. It should be inflated to a pressure where, when dropped from a height of six feet, it bounces to a height of about 4 ft 6 ins to the top of the ball.

Backboard

The backboard is made of wood painted white or a rigid transparent material such as perspex, with dimensions and markings as shown in the diagram. It should be suspended in the vertical plane with the lower edge 9 ft above the floor and 4 ft inside the end line with its centre midway between the sidelines.

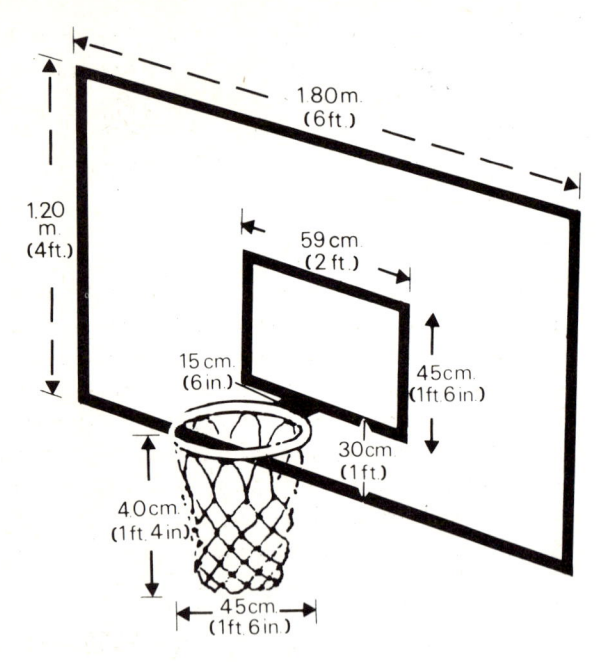

The backboard and basket

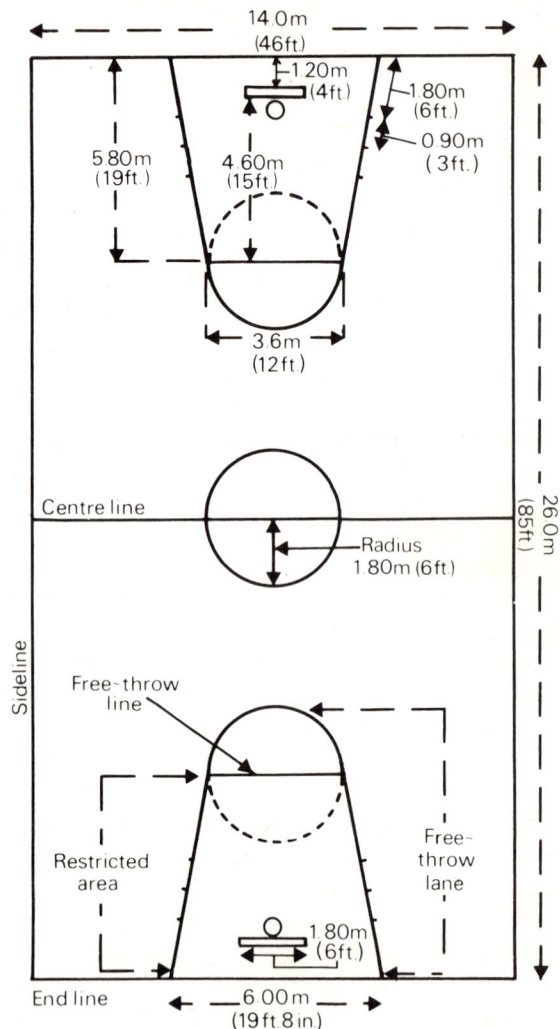

The court, with markings

Basket

The basket comprises a metal ring and bottomless net attached at right angles to the backboard, with dimensions as shown in the diagram. The ring should be painted orange and have an inside diameter of 18 ins. Its thickness should be about ¾ in. The net should be slightly tapered so as to slow the ball without stopping it. The ring should be attached to the backboard as shown, exactly 10 ft from the ground.

Court

The court is rectangular with markings and dimensions as shown in the diagram. Its width can vary by 3 ft and its length by 6 ft, as long as the proportion is maintained. It can be made of any suitably hard material but the favoured surface is wood.

THE RULES IN DETAIL

Kit

Shirt, shorts and boots with numbers on front and back of shorts.

Officials

Each game should have two referees, dividing the court between them and exchanging places after every incident. Whistles and hand signals are used to explain decisions. (see referee diagrams p. 42). They are assisted by the scorer, timekeeper and 30-second operator. The scorer carries five markers, numbered 1-4 in black, 5 in red, to indicate the number of fouls per player. There is also a larger red marker, numbered 8, to show when a team has reached eight team fouls.

THE GAME

The visitors choose ends, or if on a neutral court

the sides toss a coin. Ends change at half-time. Play begins with a jump ball.

Scoring

Points are scored two ways: baskets (field goals) and foul shots. Baskets are scored when the ball goes through the ring from anywhere on court and always counts two points. A foul shot can be scored only when an official awards shots from the foul line, which is positioned exactly 15 feet in front of the basket, and always counts one point for each shot made. Free throws must be taken by the player who was fouled. In the case of technical fouls (see later), any player may attempt the throw.

Interference

Shots at goal cannot be blocked on the downward path above the level of the ring until the ball has touched the ring. Violations by the defending team result in two points for the opposition, while violations by the offensive team result in a sideline throw-in.

Restarting the game

After a field goal or free throws, play restarts with a throw-in from the end line by the defending team.

After loss of possession or ball out of bounds, play is restarted with a throw-in on the sideline nearest the infraction.

In all cases, the clock starts when the ball touches a player on court or, in the case of a jump ball, when the ball is first tapped.

Duration

There are two halves of 20 minutes, with the clock stopped every time the whistle is blown. It is not restarted until the last foul shot (free throw) is taken or, in the case of throw-ins, until the ball reaches the first recipient. If the score is tied at the end of normal time, play continues for as many extra five-minute periods as it takes to produce a result.

Jump ball

The game starts with the referee throwing the ball up in the centre circle. Two opposing players only are allowed in this area, each standing in the half nearest their own basket with one foot touching the centre line. Each player is allowed two taps to get the ball to a team-mate before it touches the ground. A jump ball also takes place if the ball becomes dead with neither team in possession.

Play

The ball can be advanced by passing or dribbling. The dribble consists of using either hand to bounce the ball, but never both hands at the same time. Once a player has stopped his dribble and picked up the ball, he cannot resume his dribble or take further steps unless he first passes or shoots. Other permitted methods of play are batting, tapping and rolling the ball, but not punching, kicking or carrying it.

Ball out of bounds

Whenever a player holding the ball touches the boundary line, the ball is considered out of bounds and possession is awarded to the other side. A ball is not out of bounds until it either hits the floor or strikes an object outside the court area. Play is restarted with a throw-in.

Offence and defence

The centre line divides the court into a team's defensive and offensive ends. The basket towards which a team shoots is its offensive end while the basket it defends is its defensive end. Once a team crosses the centre line into its offensive end, it cannot move the ball back over the centre line.

Time-out

Each side may call two one-minute breaks per half. These are known as charged time-outs and may be taken by coaches if they want to alter tactics or break the opposition's rhythm. One time-out per side is allowed in each period of extra time. Other time-outs may be called by the referees to deal with injuries etc and in all cases the clock is stopped. When play is ready to resume, the referee will signal time-in.

3-second rule

No player, with or without the ball, may remain more than 3 seconds inside the key-shaped area under his offensive end's basket when his side are in possession. The defensive team may remain in the key for as long it likes.

30-second rule
A team must try a shot within 30 seconds of gaining possession or forfeit possession.

10-second rule
A team in possession in its defensive half must advance the ball over the centre line within ten seconds or forfeit possession.

THE REFEREE'S SIGNALS

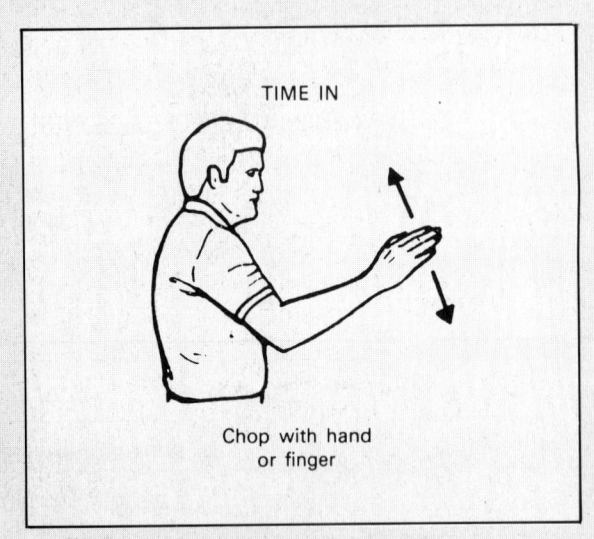

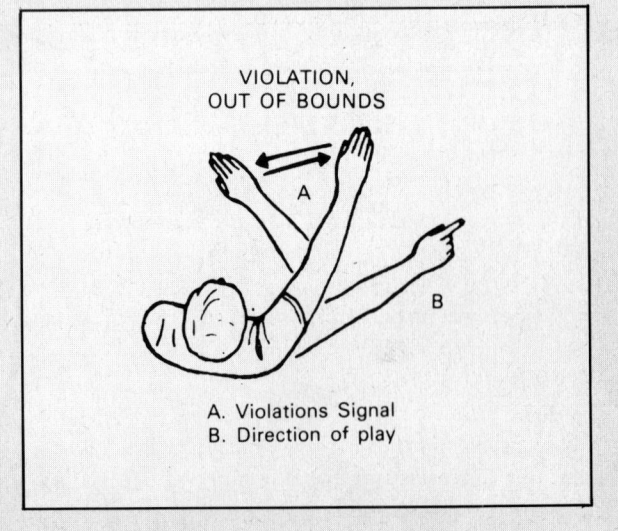

CHARGED TIME-OUT
Form T, finger showing

TIME IN
Chop with hand or finger

SUBSTITUTION
Crossing forearms

OFFICIAL'S TIME-OUT
Open Palm

VIOLATION, OUT OF BOUNDS
A. Violations Signal
B. Direction of play

RULES OF THE GAME 43

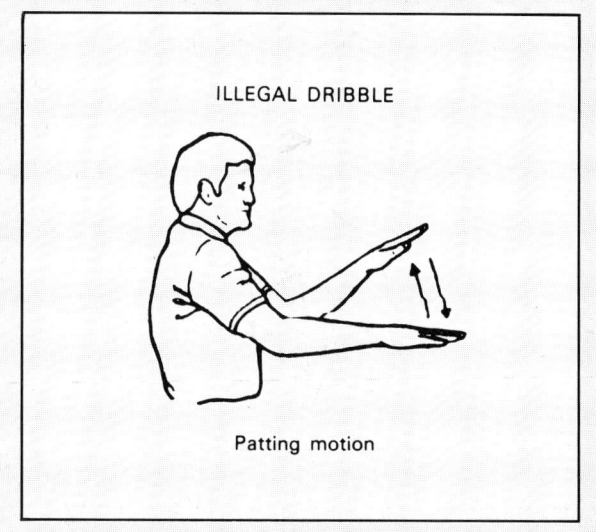

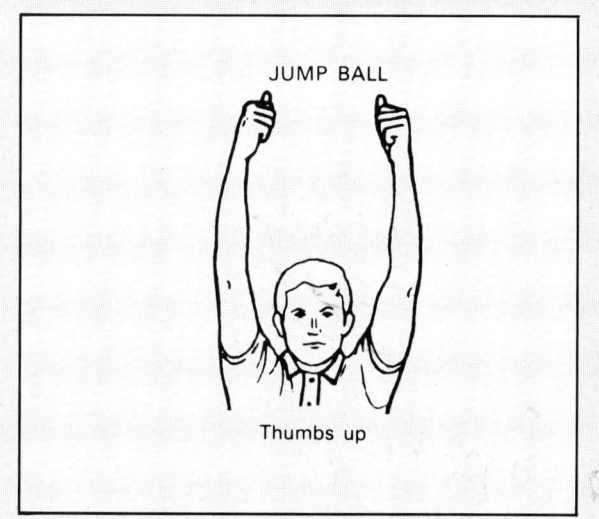

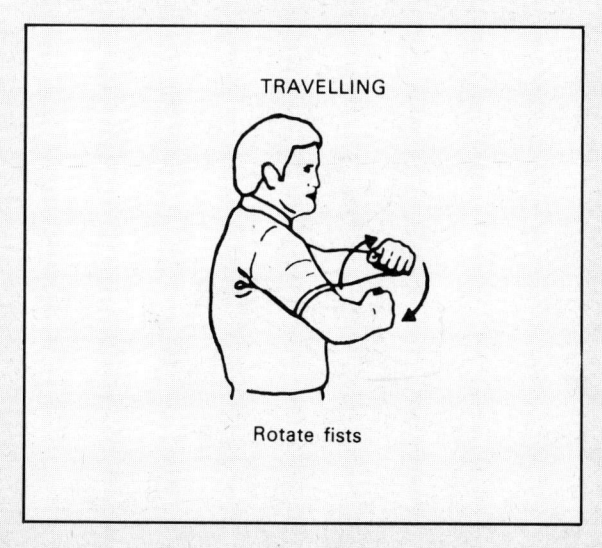

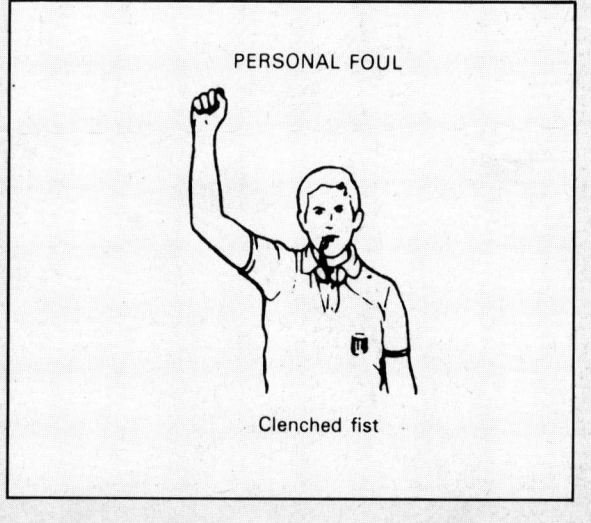

ILLEGAL DRIBBLE	3-SECOND RULE INFRACTION
Patting motion	Fingers sideways
JUMP BALL	FREE THROWS PENALTY
Thumbs up	Fingers pointing to free throw line, followed by signal of the number of free throws.
TRAVELLING	PERSONAL FOUL
Rotate fists	Clenched fist

44 DAN LLOYD'S BOOK OF BASKETBALL

TECHNICAL FOUL 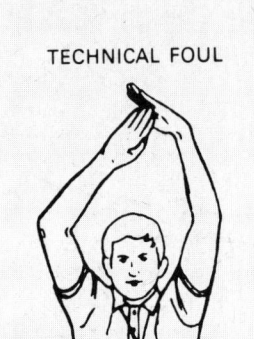
Form T, Palm showing

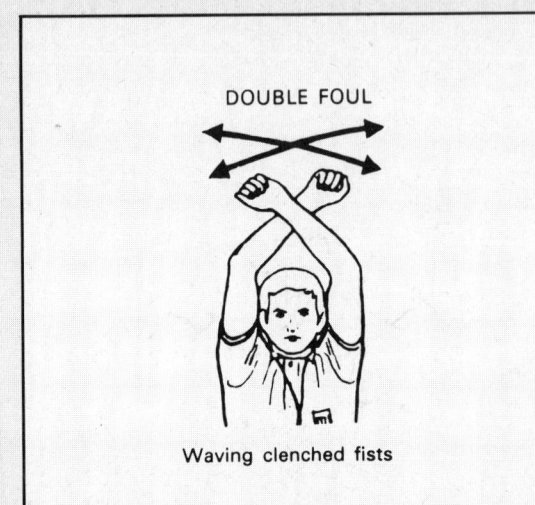

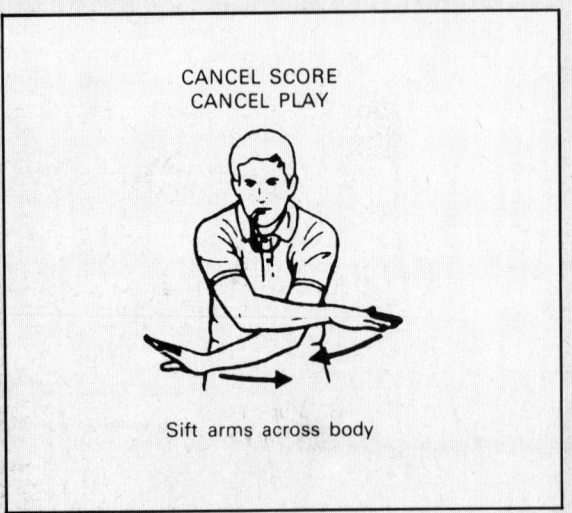

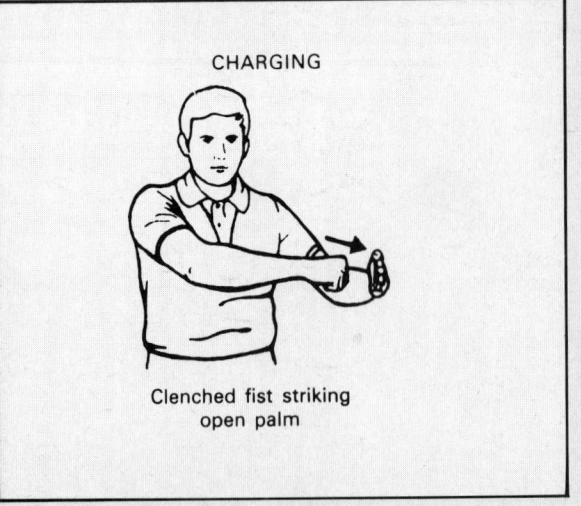

DOUBLE FOUL
Waving clenched fists

CANCEL SCORE CANCEL PLAY
Sift arms across body

INTENTIONAL FOUL
Grasp wrist

PERSONAL FOUL
No free throws
Finger pointing to side line

CHARGING
Clenched fist striking open palm

RULES OF THE GAME 45

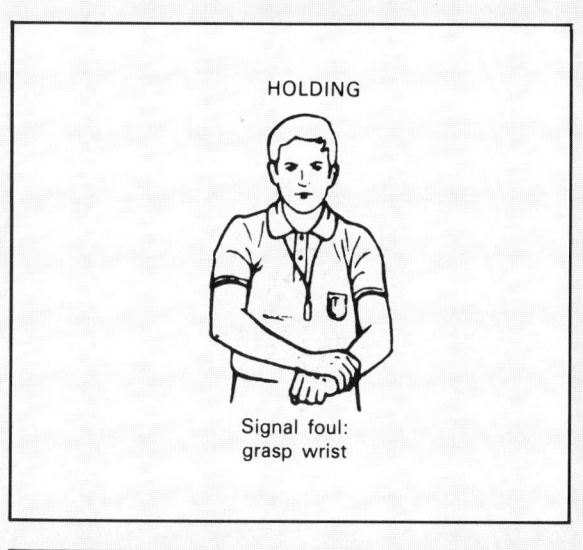

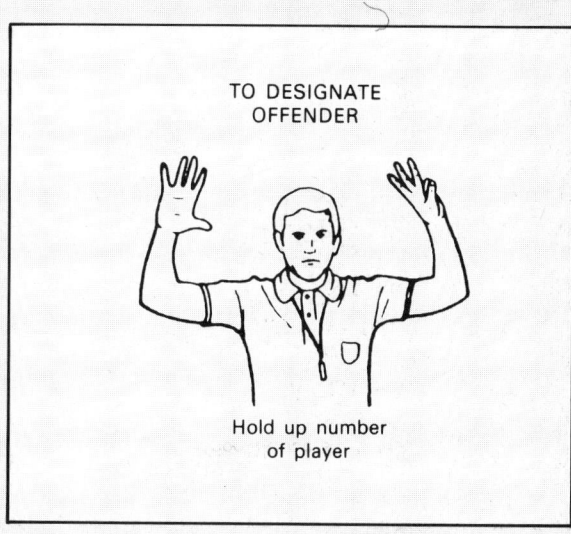

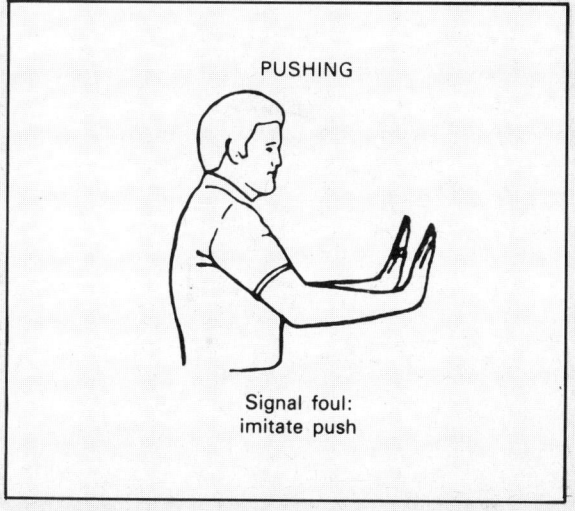

FOUL BY TEAM IN CONTROL OF THE BALL
Both hands on hips

ILLEGAL USE OF HANDS
Signal foul: strike wrist

HOLDING
Signal foul: grasp wrist

TO DESIGNATE OFFENDER
Hold up number of player

PUSHING
Signal foul: imitate push

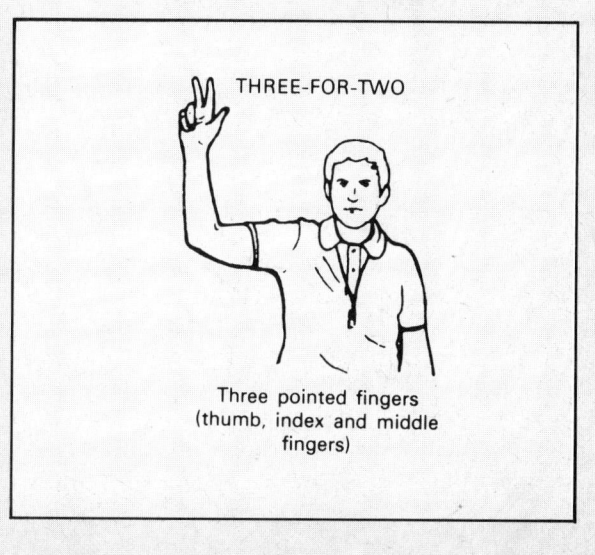

THREE-FOR-TWO
Three pointed fingers (thumb, index and middle fingers)

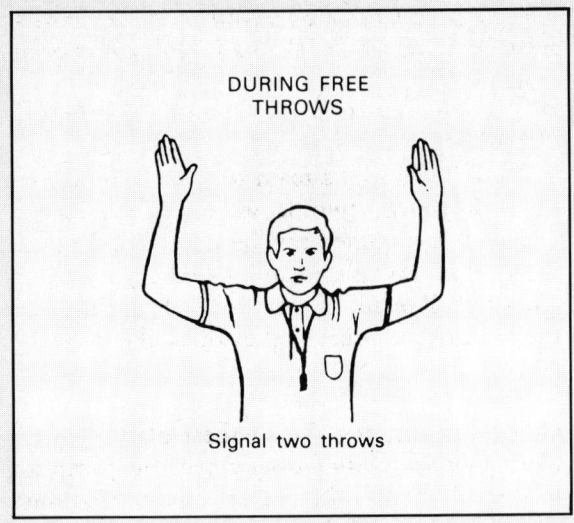

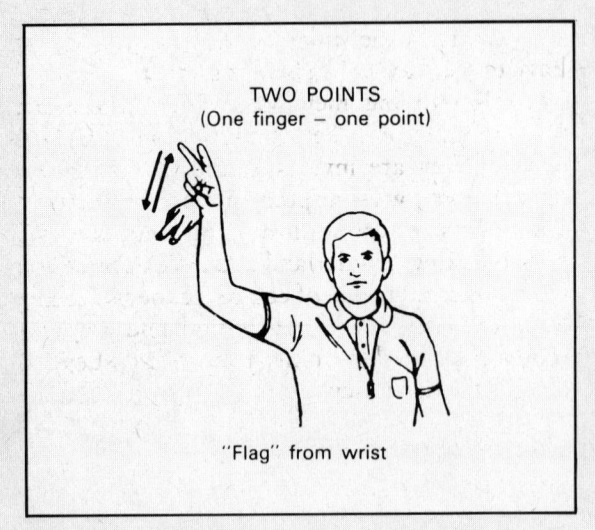

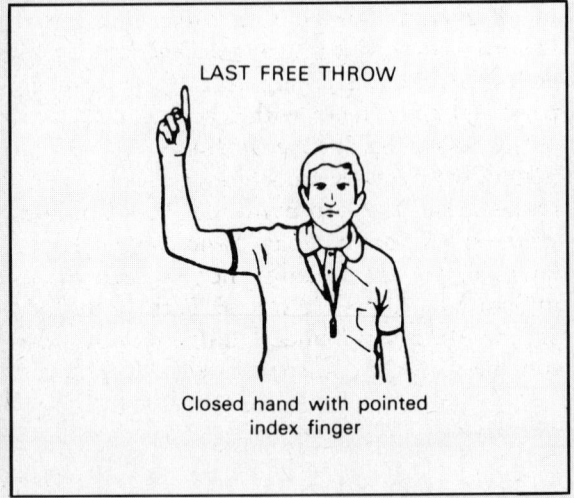

DURING FREE THROWS
Signal when no rebound situation can follow

DURING FREE THROWS
Signal two throws

TWO POINTS
(One finger – one point)
"Flag" from wrist

LAST FREE THROW
Closed hand with pointed index finger

FOULS

Basketball is theoretically a non-contact sport but in reality it has a strong physical element. However, contact such as holding, pushing, charging, tripping or otherwise impeding an opponent is penalised. If a player is fouled in the act of shooting, he is awarded one or more free shots from the free-throw line, depending on whether his original attempt was successful or not. If it was, he is awarded one free shot for one extra point. If not, he is awarded three attempts to score two points, each successful shot counting one point each.

Fouls that take place when players are not in the act of shooting, together with other rule infractions such as illegal dribbling or running with the ball, result in loss of possession.

Technical fouls

Ungentlemanly conduct by a coach or player, such as offensive language, is penalised by two free throws for one point each by the opposition.

Personal fouls

Each player is allowed up to five fouls of any sort; on the fifth he is automatically disqualified. A substitute is still allowed to take his place.

Team fouls

Each side is allowed a total of up to eight fouls

per half before every subsequent offence against the team in control of the ball results in two free throws.

POSITIONS

The starting five of a team will normally consist of two guards, two forwards and a centre, although the names can be confusing because the guards don't guard and, like everyone else in a basketball team, the forwards play as much at the back of the court as they do at the front.

Guards

Guards are usually the smallest players of the five, in many cases proving a brilliant exception to the rule that basketball is a sport for giants. Their principal qualities are ball-handling, quickness and shooting ability. One guard, known as the point guard, will be team general, or 'play-maker', bringing the ball up court and triggering the offence with a pinpoint pass or a defence-splitting dribble. It's usually a position held down by Americans because they have the requisite skills. Alton Byrd and Russ Saunders, whose talents are compared and contrasted in a later chapter, are probably the two finest guards in British basketball, but Karl Tatham (Solent), Jimmy Macauley (Sunderland) and John Johnson (Solent) herald the new breed of Englishmen snapping at their heels. The other guard will also be a good ball-handler and one of the best scorers in the side. This is one of the positions usually held by English players in the NBL, with Crystal Palace's Paul Stimpson the outstanding example.

Forwards

Forwards are in the intermediate height range, usually between 6 ft 4 ins and 6 ft 9 ins and are expected to defend and score with equal consistency. One forward is usually a good jumper and outside shooter, such as England's Pete Jeremich, while the other will be a good rebounder and close-to-the-basket scorer.

The centre

The centre is the pillar of the side. You only have to see players like Solent's Mark Saiers and Palace's two big men Mike Spaid and Greg McGray to appreciate the importance of a good centre. They are invariably the tallest players on the team, with responsibilities for offensive and defensive rebounding, inside shooting and shot-blocking. Sunderland's Art Wearren differs from the usual image of centres as the incredible hulks of basketball. Wearren is tall and wiry and scores most of his points from jump shots of devastating accuracy.

5 England on the Move

Istanbul will go down as a watershed in England's international history. The year was 1981 and the event was a European championship match which would determine whether England remained in the international wilderness or rose into the ranks of teams to be respected. From a position outside Europe's top 30 at the start of the year, England had progressed into the top 20. Victory against Turkey would clinch a place in the top 12.

For England this was far more than a game of basketball. It was a confrontation in which the most essential qualities of the national team – character and determination – were put to their stiffest-ever test.

There was little indication of the turbulence to come as England took an early lead. But as they settled down into what looked like a winning pattern, the home crowd became more and more hostile.

The first incident came when England scored a particularly good basket: a drinks can hit the floor of the gymnasium. Then another and another. Suddenly the air was thick with metal. As the England bench looked round from the edge of the court, it was to see 12,000 Turks and not a friendly face among them.

The floor was cleared and the game continued. But within a few minutes more cans were raining down and again the game had to be stopped. This happened repeatedly, even after police were called. As a result England's rhythm was upset and the Turks edged their way back.

England went into half-time 14 points ahead and then there was more trouble. The scoreboard broke down and the police insisted the game should not restart until the crowd had settled. When the game did get going again, the England players were cold from standing around and the 14-point lead melted away in a matter of some four minutes.

England called a time-out, rallied their team and went back into a healthy lead. Then more crowd trouble broke out and this time the army was called in.

Bill Beswick, assistant to England coach Vic Ambler at the time, has a vivid memory of the occasion: 'Here we were in Istanbul playing a basketball match against Turkey and the entire court was ringed with soldiers facing out away from the game with their guns pointing into the crowd.'

At this point it was announced that if one more incident occurred, the game would be called off and awarded to England. That seemed to work like magic on the Turkish crowd. The scores were level but Turkey were on eight team fouls. England instructed their guards, Paul Stimpson and Karl Tatham, to drive for the basket whenever possible to try to draw fouls.

'What always stands out in my memory,' says Beswick 'is that the last eight points were scored by England from the free-throw line under enormous pressure – and all by Paul Stimpson.

'The crowd were hissing, jeering and stamping their feet and I can always recall Stimpson's face and the little look he gave towards our bench. It was just the slightest of winks, and everyone knew than that he was in control of himself and that character would win.'

Stimpson scored eight out of eight, England won, the troops rushed them to their dressing-room and the police escorted the crowd out while the players just sat exhausted, knowing that they'd done it.

OPPOSITE: *England's Pete Mullings prepares for a free shot*

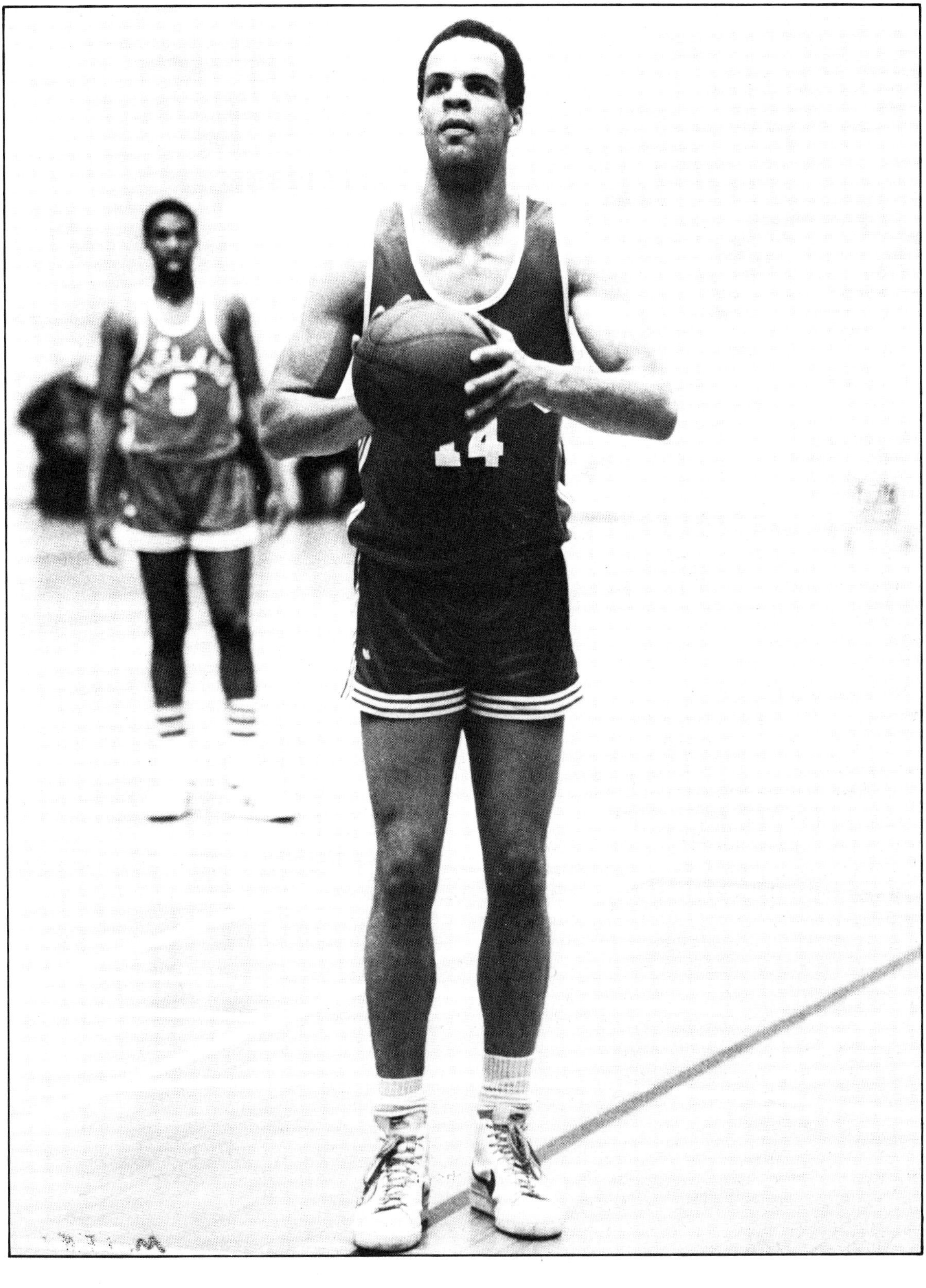

'I must just add,' Beswick continued, 'that when we took the team to the bazaar for shopping next day, the people there couldn't have been nicer, and the old saying that when the game's over, the game's over, was absolutely true.'

Indeed that victory turned the Turks into England fans for their next game a couple of days later. A great cheer went up from another huge crowd of around 12,000 when the team began their warming-up routine.

But the players were puzzled when the fans began chanting: 'Kunta Kinte! Kunta Kinte!' Jimmy Macauley, one of the jokers in the team, immediately raised his arms. But his coffee-coloured skin obviously wasn't dark enough. There were a few catcalls and whistles.

Then Karl Tatham made his bow. The applause was thunderous. 'They must have been showing the Turkish version of *Roots* on television,' says Beswick. 'Karl was the only black player in the championships and the Turks had obviously taken a shine to him.'

Beswick, who took over as national coach in 1983 from Tom Wisman (Ambler's successor), believes that three factors have accelerated England's rise in recent years: the finance which has enabled the national team to undertake a more competitive and far-reaching programme; a better standard of player available, mainly through the arrival of dual nationals to play in the English league; and the higher quality of coaches at all levels from the senior men's coach to the youngest boys' team.

More money has come into the game mainly as a result of the formation of the national league; dual nationals of high calibre arrived as a result of clubs seeking out English players who had learned their basketball in the United States; and the improvement in coaching standards came with the growth of the league and the knowledge and expertise which the expansion spawned.

Beswick pays tribute to the work and achievements of Vic Ambler, who presided over England's transformation between 1971 and 1981 and had the satisfaction of retiring with the national team at their highest-ever ranking of eleventh after the final European championship round in Prague. 'It was,' says Beswick, 'a magnificent achievement.' Beswick is confident that despite a lapse in the 1982 championships, England can build on their earlier successes:

'I'm optimistic because the national programme has taken great strides forward in recent years and I have a better starting-point. I'm also optimistic because of the quality of the English players being produced by the national league, and by the quality of the league itself, which can now be compared with some of the best in Europe. The stronger the domestic competition, the stronger the national team.'

However, Beswick sees two major problems: a danger that any expansion of the league programme could be made at the expense of the national programme, thus possibly producing a conflict of interest between club and country; and the growing disparity between what the national set-up can offer in terms of subsidies to players who agree to undertake sometimes lengthy international tours, and what clubs may offer as an alternative attraction.

A more immediate problem for Beswick is how to maintain a happy medium between his dual national players and his England-produced players. In theory it would be possible to pick an England team comprising solely dual nationals. But Beswick stresses the importance of a symbiosis between the two: 'The American influence on the game has been very strong and very necessary in developing our game so rapidly. I have always viewed it as being of assistance to our game but I do get concerned at times that instead of just support, it might emerge as a takeover.

'I feel that there must always be room in the national team for English players who have gone through the system and that we can look back with pride on the efforts of the families, school teachers, youth coaches and club coaches who have produced international players like Paul Stimpson.

'So the rise of the dual national and the development of the English player must go hand-in-hand, and they each owe a great deal to the other.'

OPPOSITE: *John Johnson in action against Austria*

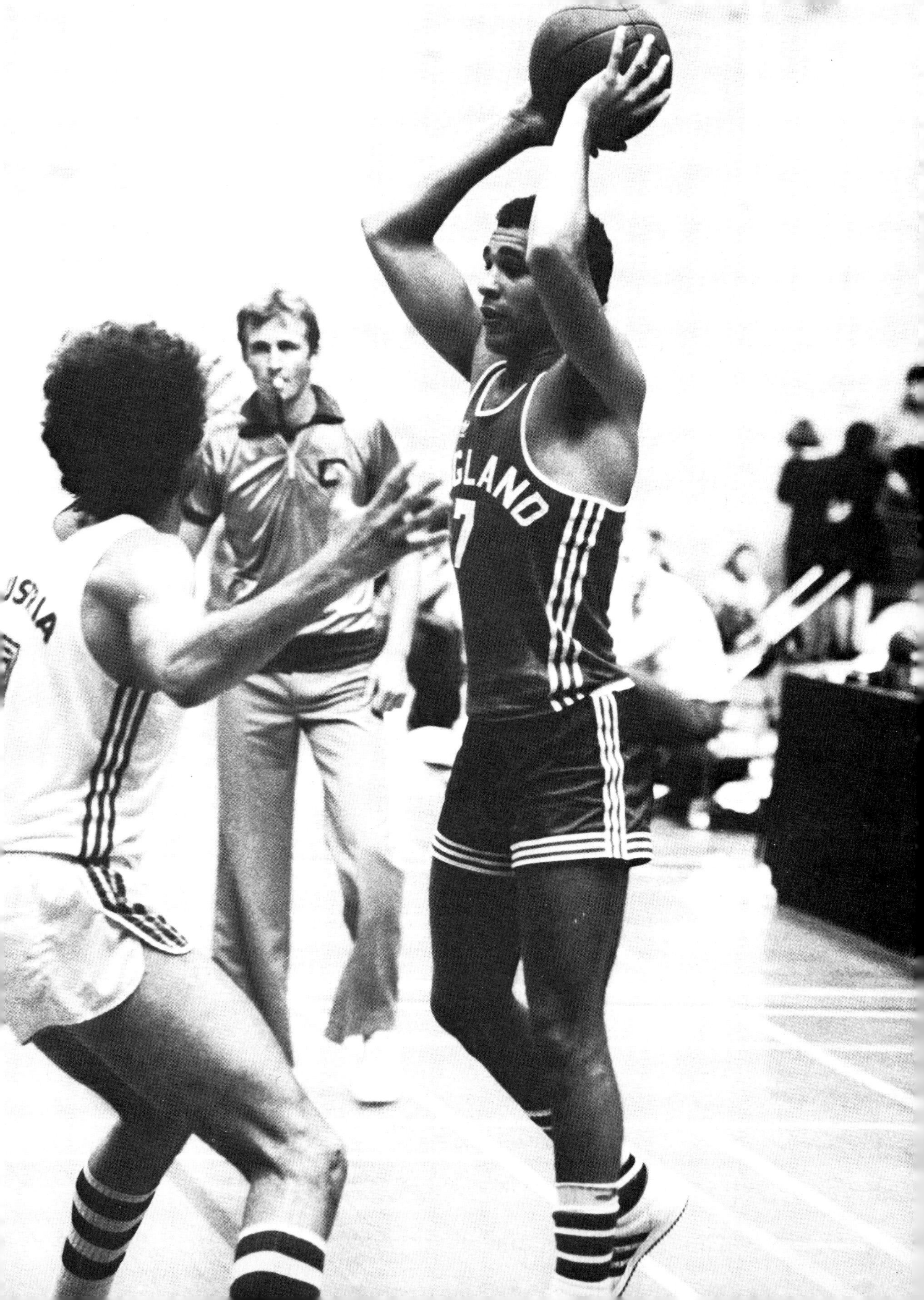
GLAND

ABOVE: *Paul Richards plays in a leg brace to protect a weak knee*   OPPOSITE: *England veteran Ian Day*

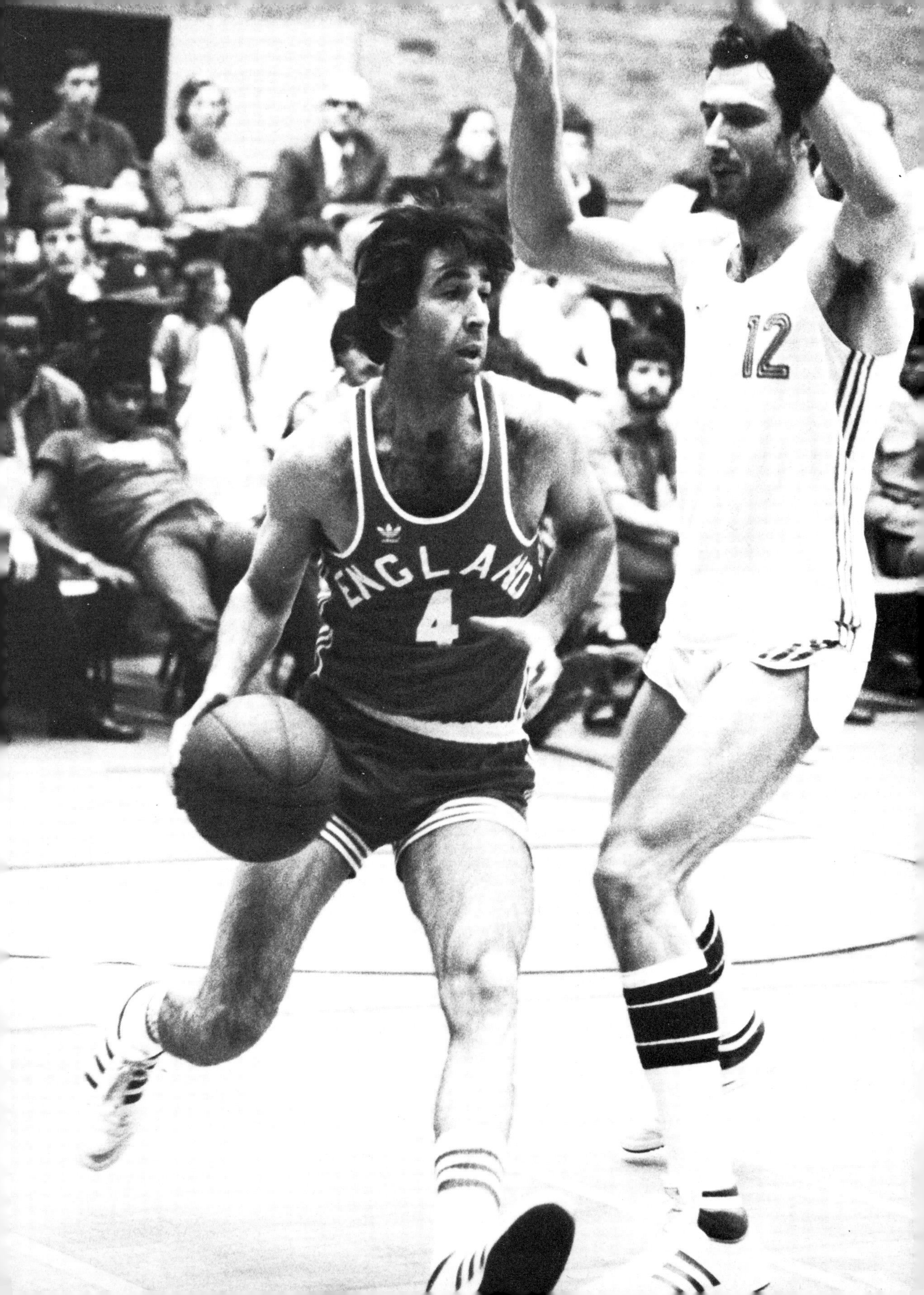
ENGLAND
4
12

6 Stars of the Eighties

Comments by Dan Lloyd

Steve Assinder (GB) *6 ft 4 ins guard. Teams: Birmingham and England.*
A scrapper. Doesn't have a lot of physical talent but his outstanding quality is that he hates to lose, and when I hear a player say that, I like to have him on my side.

Jimmy Brandon (US) *6 ft 5 ins forward. Team: Sunderland.*
A hustler. Does a lot of things you don't notice and takes a lot of rebounds. He's not a good shooter but he's good on defence and stays with his man well.

Jim Brandon

Tom Broderick (US) *6 ft 6 ins forward. Team: Kingston.*
A big man who protects the ball well and scores from all over the court. He can also make some good moves to the basket and shows good ball-handling.

Vince Brookins (US) *6 ft 6 ins forward. Team: Manchester.*
Nobody who saw his powerhouse performance for Sunderland against Solent in the 1982 championship semi-finals is likely to forget Vince in a hurry. A great shooter and rebounder with the muscle to frighten any team.

Alton Byrd (US) *5 ft 8 ins guard. Team: Murray.*
A great loss to Palace and the NBL when he went to Edinburgh because he is one of the few players who can take control of a game rather than have to adapt to someone else's game. His other attributes are his ball-handling, his quickness and, for a small player, his shooting.

Larry Dassie (US) *6 ft 6 ins forward. Team: Hemel Hempstead..*
One of the most exciting players I've seen. He's a good offensive rebounder who scores a lot of points inside. Always plays hard and wants to win.

Ian Day (GB) *6 ft 4 ins guard. Teams: Doncaster and England.*
A player who uses his wide experience in critical situations. Not a particularly good ball player, which detracts from his overall effectiveness, but an excellent shooter – reflected in the stats where he's the league's all-time leading scorer.

ALTON BYRD

FULL NAME: Joseph Alton Byrd
DATE OF BIRTH: 3 November 1957
PLACE OF BIRTH: San Francisco, California, USA
BROUGHT UP: San Francisco
HEIGHT: 5 ft 8 ins
WEIGHT: 11 stone 11 lb
CAR: Audi Coupé 5S
CLUBS: Crystal Palace, Murray Edinburgh
GREATEST MOMENT: Far too many to count
WORST MOMENT: As above
FAVOURITE OTHER PLAYER: Mark Saiers
ALL-TIME BEST NBL LINE-UP: Mark Saiers, Jimmie Guymon, Vince Brookins, Alton Byrd, Joe Pace
FAVOURITE FOOD/DRINK: Steak, milk shakes
FAVOURITE FILM/TV PROGRAMME: One Flew Over the Cuckoo's Nest, Panorama, Kenny Everett
FAVOURITE MUSIC: Jazz, fusion jazz, bee-bop jazz
FAVOURITE READING: *Sports Illustrated*, *Financial Times*, autobiographies
SUPERSTITIONS: None
WHAT WOULD YOU LIKE TO HAVE BEEN IF NOT A BASKETBALL PLAYER? Investment analyst

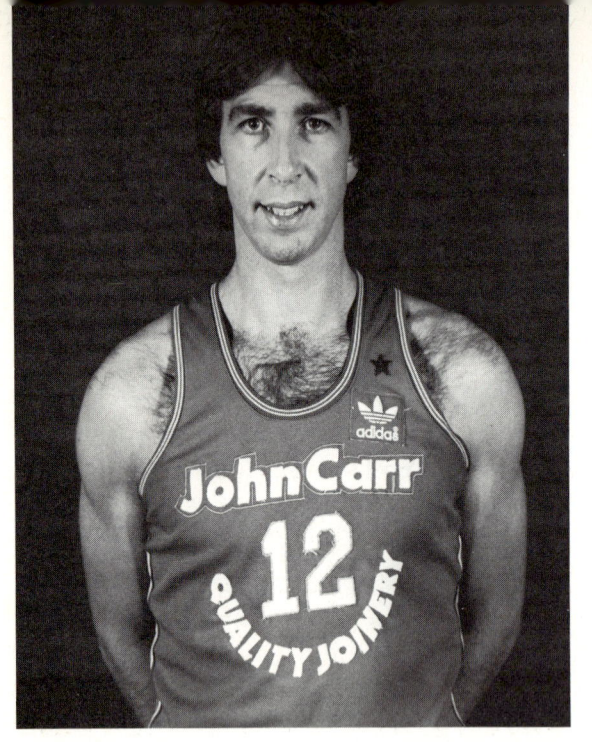

Ian Day

Clive Hartley

John Johnson

Dip Donaldson (US/dual national) 6 ft 7 ins forward. Team: Birmingham.
Has improved his scoring potential by going in low to the basket as well as shooting from further out. A good jumper and rebounder.

Clive Hartley (GB) 6 ft 5 ins forward. Teams: Sunderland and England.
If he can improve his confidence, he has the ability to become a fine player. He has a good quick first step to the basket but it's the finishing touch which lets him down – he's not quite sure what to do.

Neville Hopkins (GB) 6 ft 9 ins centre. Teams: Birmingham and England.
Limited in ability but makes up for it by being efficient. He's one of the better taller English players who rebounds well and does a lot which doesn't always show up on the stats.

John Johnson (GB) 6 ft 3 ins guard Teams: Solent and England.
Excellent one-to-one player. Probably the best scorer in the game in that he's equally good inside and out, and can also post down smaller and bigger players.

STARS OF THE EIGHTIES 57

David Lloyd (*US/dual national*) 6 ft 4 ins forward. Teams: Hemel Hempstead and England.
Too short to be an out-and-out shooting forward but a very valuable player in all departments: rebounding, blocking and scoring important points.

Doug Lloyd (*US/dual national*) 6 ft 6 ins forward. Team: Kingston.
He can be a really good all-round player, one of the best in the NBL if he puts his mind to it. Back home he's always been rated the most talented of us three but he needs the right coach to bring that out.

Jimmy Macauley (*GB*) 6 ft 3 ins guard. Teams: Sunderland and England.
I rated him when I first saw him with Milton Keynes. Not the most steady of guards because he is not that good a ball-handler, but he is able to score from some very difficult situations and draws a lot of charging fouls.

Ken Kocher

Jeff Jones (*US*) 6 ft 4 ins guard. Team: Warrington.
A good, offensive player who scores from inside and outside. He has a good range for his jump-shooting but he treats defence as just another part of the game.

Steve Keenan (*US*) 6 ft 7 ins forward. Team: Bracknell.
Not the fastest of players but a good rebounder with good inside skills and one of the league's nice guys.

Ken Kocher (*GB*) 6 ft 5 ins forward. Team: Sunderland.
A good battler and rebounder. Most of his points are going to come from inside because he doesn't have the range, but he uses his strength to post down low, close to the basket.

Lonnie Legette (*US*) 6 ft 1 in. guard. Team: Leicester.
A very smooth player who has the advantage for a guard of being a good jumper for his height. As well as being a good outside shooter, he can go inside opponents to shoot, or jump over them.

Jimmy Macauley

Greg McCray (US) *6 ft 6 ins forward. Team: Crystal Palace.*
Excellent inside player, particularly defensively. Good hands so that you know whenever you throw him the ball he's not going to lose it. Rebounds well and has improved his shooting.

Rodney McKeever (US) *6 ft guard. Team: Bolton.*
One of the star turns of the Second Division in 1982–83. A good shooter who gets up very high for a small guy. It should be interesting to see how he matches up in the First Division, especially against players like Russ Saunders.

Pete Mullings (US/dual national) *6 ft 9 ins centre. Teams: Sunderland and England.*
A good rebounder and sound defensive player. Never criticizes his team-mates on court, which I feel is the sign of a good team player. Hustles well but can only score from close in.

Ken Nottage (GB) *6 ft 3 ins guard. Team: Sunderland.*
A good ball player who has improved tremendously in the last four years. He makes some nice drives to the basket as well as hitting a good jump shot. In time I think he'll make an outstanding England guard.

Ken Pemberton (US/dual national) *6 ft 6 ins centre. Team: Leicester.*
An excellent offensive and defensive rebounder. Not a good shooter or ball-handler but very smart around the basket and always hustling.

Paul Philp (GB) *6 ft 1 in. guard. Teams: Solent and England.*
A left-handed player who's very experienced and who always seems to hurt you. You can shut down other players but he always seems to come on and score just when you don't want him to. Good defence and hustles well.

Paul Richards (US/dual national) *6 ft 9 ins forward. Teams: Kingston and England.*
Not a quick player because he has to play with a leg brace but he's very smart defensively and draws a lot of charges. A good outside shooter.

Paul Philp

Paul Richards

KEN PEMBERTON

FULL NAME: Kenneth Wayne Pemberton
DATE OF BIRTH: 23 August 1956
PLACE OF BIRTH: White Earth, Minnesota, USA
BROUGHT UP: Same place, till 17
HEIGHT: 6 ft 6 ins
WEIGHT: 14 stone 9 lb
CAR: Alfa Romeo (here's hoping!)
PREVIOUS CLUBS: Kingston, Hemel Hempstead, Solent, Leicester
GREATEST MOMENT: Too many to remember
WORST MOMENT: Failure to qualify for Wembley with Leicester in 1983
ALL-TIME BEST NBL LINE-UP: Alton Byrd, Lonnie Legette, Larry Dassie, Joe Pace, Bobby Cooper
MOST PROMISING YOUNG PLAYER: Steve O'Shea (Leicester)
FAVOURITE FOOD/DRINK: Seafood. I drink whatever people will give me; I'm usually too thirsty to be choosy
FAVOURITE MUSIC: Love and dance music
FAVOURITE FILM/TV PROGRAMME: Cool Hand Luke starring Paul Newman, any comedies or documentaries
FAVOURITE READING: History
SUPERSTITIONS: None
WHAT WOULD YOU LIKE TO HAVE BEEN IF NOT A BASKETBALL PLAYER? An American pro footballer

T. J. Robinson

Drew Sewell

T.J. Robinson (US) *6 ft 8 ins centre. Team: Solent.*
At his best, he's awesome. Rebounds well and scores well, but at other times he doesn't make that much impact. If he could become more consistent, he'd be a great player.

Mark Saiers (US) *6 ft 8 ins centre. Team: Solent.*
The type of player anyone would want on their side. A great defensive player who positions himself so well that he's always there to pick up the rebounds. His only drawback is that he doesn't look to shoot as often as he should which can be a disadvantage if his side are looking for points late in a game.

Russ Saunders (US) *5 ft 11 ins. Team: Birmingham.*
One of the best guards in the league. Can score going to the basket, shoots well from outside and good defence – a complete ball player.

Drew Sewell (GB) *6 ft 5 ins forward. Teams: Hemel Hempstead and England.*
Young left-handed player who improves every game. Drives well to the basket and hustles a lot, but he needs to work on his right hand if he's not to become too predictable.

Dave Shelley (GB) *5 ft 10 ins guard. Teams: Hemel Hempstead and England.*
One of the best English guards but he hasn't improved as much as I thought he would. Good steady ball player who doesn't make too many mistakes considering the pressure he's always under. Good jump shooter.

Mike Spaid (US/dual national) *6 ft 10 ins. Team: Crystal Palace.*
Impresses me more every time I see him. Excellent rebounder who uses his strength and size well. Good scorer close to the basket. If he qualifies for the England team, he'll be a great addition.

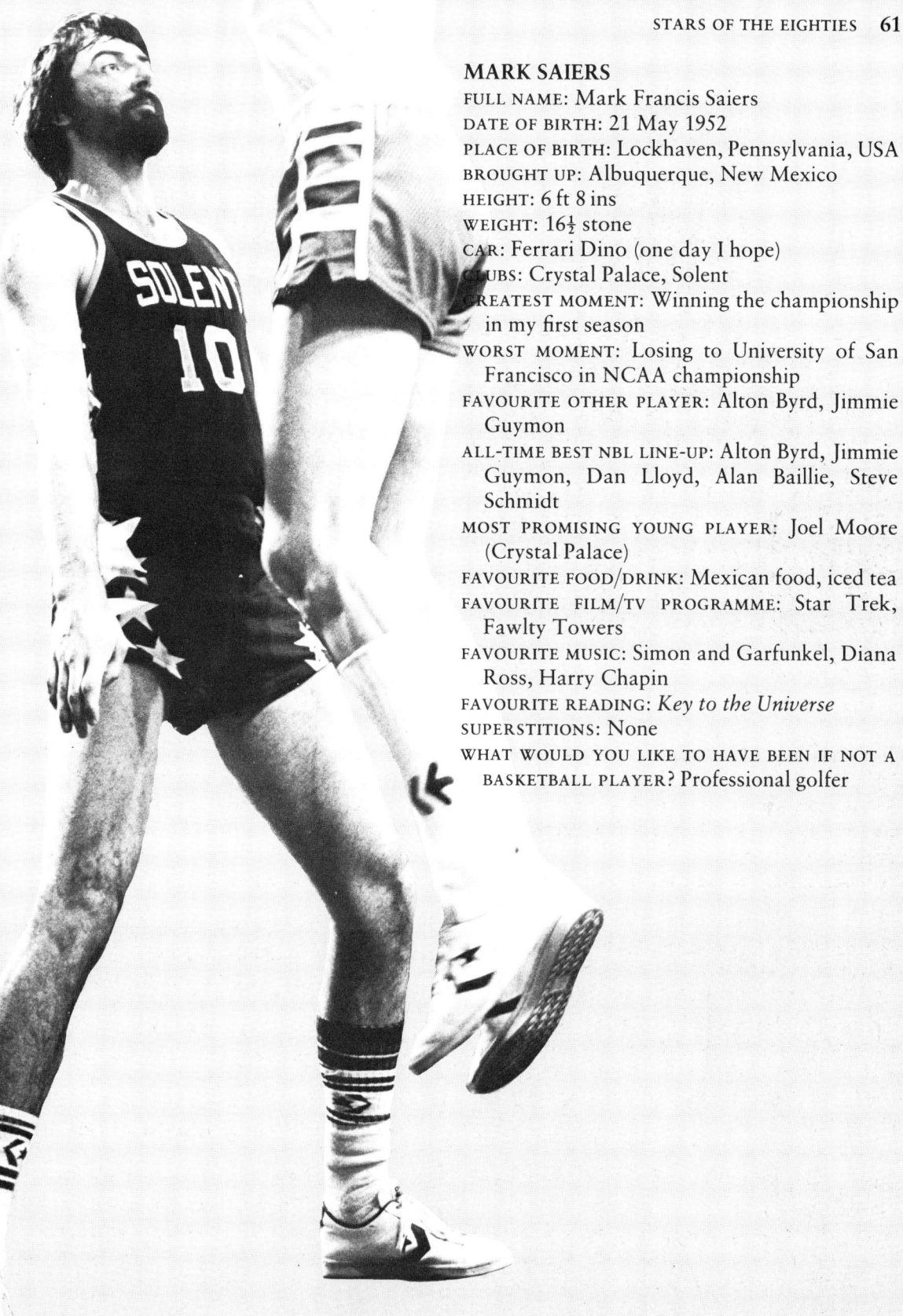

MARK SAIERS

FULL NAME: Mark Francis Saiers
DATE OF BIRTH: 21 May 1952
PLACE OF BIRTH: Lockhaven, Pennsylvania, USA
BROUGHT UP: Albuquerque, New Mexico
HEIGHT: 6 ft 8 ins
WEIGHT: 16½ stone
CAR: Ferrari Dino (one day I hope)
CLUBS: Crystal Palace, Solent
GREATEST MOMENT: Winning the championship in my first season
WORST MOMENT: Losing to University of San Francisco in NCAA championship
FAVOURITE OTHER PLAYER: Alton Byrd, Jimmie Guymon
ALL-TIME BEST NBL LINE-UP: Alton Byrd, Jimmie Guymon, Dan Lloyd, Alan Baillie, Steve Schmidt
MOST PROMISING YOUNG PLAYER: Joel Moore (Crystal Palace)
FAVOURITE FOOD/DRINK: Mexican food, iced tea
FAVOURITE FILM/TV PROGRAMME: Star Trek, Fawlty Towers
FAVOURITE MUSIC: Simon and Garfunkel, Diana Ross, Harry Chapin
FAVOURITE READING: *Key to the Universe*
SUPERSTITIONS: None
WHAT WOULD YOU LIKE TO HAVE BEEN IF NOT A BASKETBALL PLAYER? Professional golfer

RUSS SAUNDERS

FULL NAME: Russell Saunders
DATE OF BIRTH: 25 November 1957
PLACE OF BIRTH: Brooklyn, New York, USA
BROUGHT UP: Brooklyn
HEIGHT: 5 ft 11 ins
WEIGHT: 11 stone 1 lb
CAR: Oldsmobile Cutlass
CLUB: Birmingham
GREATEST MOMENT: Being drafted by NBA Kansas City Kings
WORST MOMENT: Losing national college championship with Pensacola in 1977
ALL-TIME BEST NBL LINE-UP: Mark Saiers, Alton Byrd, Jimmie Guymon, Ian Day, Greg White
MOST PROMISING YOUNG PLAYER: Mike Landell (Birmingham)
FAVOURITE FOOD/DRINK: Beef, O.J.
FAVOURITE FILM: The Great Gatsby
FAVOURITE MUSIC: Jazz
FAVOURITE READING: Spy books
SUPERSTITIONS: None
WHAT WOULD YOU LIKE TO HAVE BEEN IF NOT A BASKETBALL PLAYER? A businessman!

Paul Stimpson

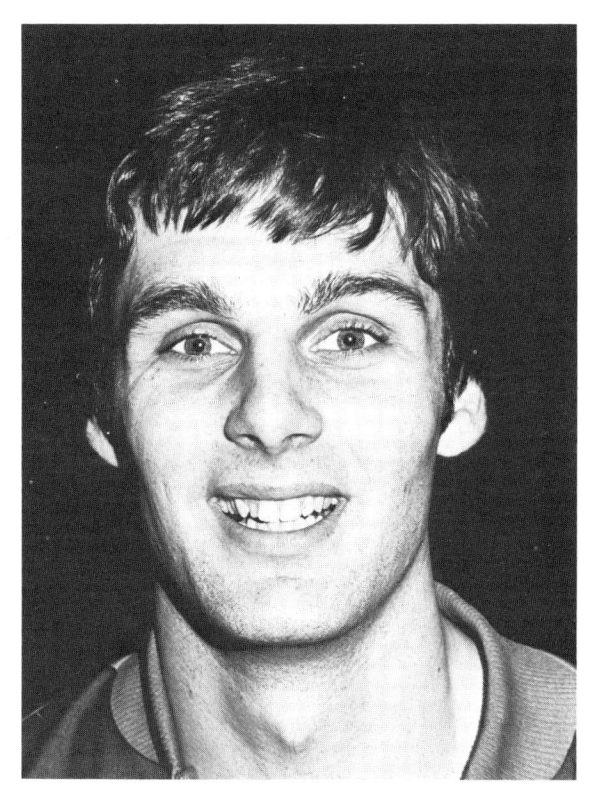

Tony Watson

Paul Stimpson (GB) *6 ft 2 ins guard. Teams: Crystal Palace and England.*
Always gives 100 per cent and puts plenty of pressure on other guards. His all-round play has improved tremendously – he drives well to the basket and can also hit some good, open jump shots.

Karl Tatham (GB) *6 ft 3 ins guard. Teams: Solent and England.*
When he's on, he's excellent. He's quick, passes well, shoots well, defends well. Creates a lot of scoring chances driving to the basket and when a man picks him up, he dumps the pass well. But to become a great player, he must learn greater consistency.

Ken Walton (GB) *6 ft 3 ins guard. Teams: Portsmouth and England.*
Good outside shooter but not a good ball-handler so he has to rely on experience. He's a physical guard and you don't find too many of those around because it's an open-court position where you need speed rather than strength. But he can defend well because he's smart and makes up for his lack of skill with his head.

Tony Watson (US/dual national) *6 ft 6 ins forward. Teams: Solent and England.*
A strong aggressive player who has improved his shooting. Excellent jumper and a good rebounder who uses all his physical attributes to the full. He can be stopped but it takes real determination!

Art Wearren (US) *6 ft 10 ins centre. Team: Sunderland.*
He would have been a pro in the US but for his lack of strength. An outstanding shooter, good passer and blocker but can be worn down because he's thin. But if he's given the room, he can be the best scoring player around from any position.

KARL TATHAM

FULL NAME: Karl Anthony Tatham
DATE OF BIRTH: 26 October 1956
PLACE OF BIRTH: London, England
BROUGHT UP: Hornsey, London, and Queens, New York City
HEIGHT: 6 ft 3 ins
WEIGHT: 13 stone 8 lb
FAMILY: My wife, Sharryl Yvette, and son Nathan Anthony
CAR: Ford Cortina
CLUB: Solent
INTERNATIONAL HONOURS: England and GB (World Student Games)
GREATEST MOMENT: Winning the Asda Cup for a second time
WORST MOMENT: Solent's performance in the 1982 championships
FAVOURITE OTHER PLAYER: Mark Saiers
ALL-TIME BEST NBL LINE-UP: Mark Saiers, Tony Watson, Alton Byrd, Bob Roma, Harvey Knuckles
MOST PROMISING YOUNG PLAYER; Joel Moore (Crystal Palace)
FAVOURITE FOOD/DRINK: Curried chicken with rice and beans, ice cream, lemonade
FAVOURITE FILM/TV PROGRAMME: Lady Sings the Blues, Brubacker, Brian's Song
FAVOURITE MUSIC: Love ballads and jazz
FAVOURITE READING: Robert Ludlum and Jeffrey Archer
SUPERSTITIONS: None
WHAT WOULD YOU LIKE TO HAVE BEEN IF NOT A BASKETBALL PLAYER? Copywriter

ART WEARREN

FULL NAME: Ardith Clay Wearren
DATE OF BIRTH: 11 November 1955
PLACE OF BIRTH: Fort Knox, Kentucky, USA
BROUGHT UP: Indianapolis, Indiana
HEIGHT: 6 ft 10 ins
WEIGHT: 14 stone
FAMILY: Three brothers, one sister
CLUBS: Montbrison, France; Racing Michelin, Belgium; La Vendeenne, France; Royal Anderlecht, Belgium, Sunderland.
GREATEST MOMENT: Winning the championship with Sunderland
WORST MOMENT: Getting a technical foul with three seconds left of a college match back home which we lost by one point
ALL-TIME BEST NBL LINE-UP: Russ Saunders, Harvey Knuckles, Dave Shutts, Jim Brandon, Art Wearren
MOST PROMISING YOUNG PLAYER: Colin Kirkham (Sunderland)
FAVOURITE FOOD/DRINK: Escalope Milanese, lasagne, French wine
FAVOURITE MUSIC: Jazz, funk, classical
FAVOURITE READING: Scientific discoveries, Philip K. Dick
SUPERSTITIONS: Always wear three pairs of wristbands and four pairs of socks
WHAT WOULD YOU LIKE TO HAVE BEEN IF NOT A BASKETBALL PLAYER? Managing director of IBM or Honeywell!

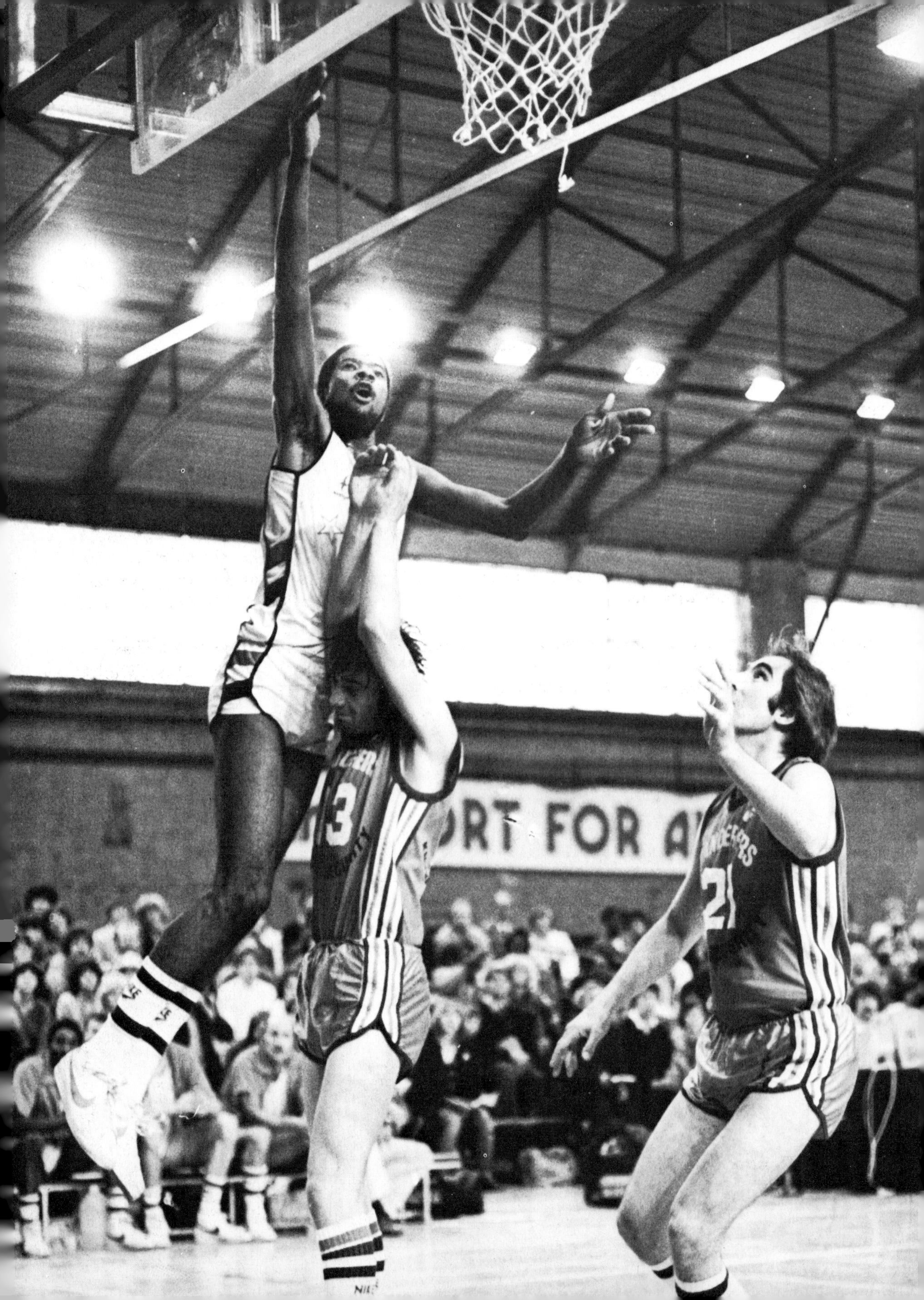
ORT FOR A

MY TOP TEN ENGLISH YOUNGSTERS

Trevor Anderson *6 ft 3 ins. Team: Crystal Palace.*
A lot of raw talent. Excellent jumper and a good rebounder who also makes a good outlet pass. The potential is there if he can develop it.

Mick Bett *6 ft 6 ins. Team: Crystal Palace.*
Very quick for a big player and an able ball-handler. Could become one of the top English players if he can become more consistent.

Winston Gordon *6 ft 5 ins. Team: Leicester.*
A good aggressive player who rebounds well but must work on his outside game because he's not big enough to pose a threat inside.

Andy Innell *6 ft 1 in. Team: Kingston.*
Makes fast, good moves to the basket but tends to dribble too high and lose the ball, which hinders his overall performance.

Colin Kirkham *6 ft 6 ins. Team: Sunderland.*
Plays aggressive defence and always gives 100 per cent. Needs to work more on his shooting and build more confidence.

Roy Lewis *6 ft 4 ins. Team: Solent.*
As a left-handed guard he's got to work more on his right. You don't see him shoot too much from outside but he drives to the basket strongly so he's always a threat.

Joel Moore *6 ft 1 in. Team: Crystal Palace.*
The best young guard around. He's very quick, a good ball-handler but needs to work on his shooting if he's to fulfil his potential.

Steve O'Shea *6 ft 4 ins. Team: Leicester.*
Another player I rated very highly when I saw him in the England squad. He's quick with good moves to the basket and shoots well. Not a very big player so he doesn't yet have the strength to hurt a team inside, so you'll usually find him on the perimeter.

Peter Scantlebury *6 ft 4 ins. Team: Bracknell.*
Much-improved player who works hard at the game. Good to see a young English player with the confidence to drive to the basket and score.

Sam Stiller *6 ft 1 in. guard. Team: Bracknell.*
Good ball-handler and shooter. Not afraid to try things, which I like to see in younger players. Has the confidence to go a long way.

Leicester's Winston Gordon, one of England's rising stars

7 Women's Scene

WOMEN'S BASKETBALL

The British Commonwealth, with the notable exception of Canada, has a 'watered down' version of basketball that is played by women and girls, as early twentieth-century female physical educationalists thought that basketball was far too robust for girls! Netball, with its limitations of speed, aggression and full-court movement, is played by most English schoolgirls. But the original, more dynamic sport of basketball is enjoyed by over seventy million athletic women all over the world and is gradually becoming accepted in schools in England. The major difference between the two games is in goal scoring: netball teams have only two shooters, whereas basketball allows everyone to 'get in on the act'.

Women's basketball is played to the same rules as the men's game. Even though the players are smaller, lighter and not as physically strong as their male counterparts, women shoot the same-sized ball into the same ten-foot-high ring, and play on the same-sized court; they employ the same tactics and use the same terminology, even to the extent of using man-to-man defence!

Internationally, women's basketball has been dominated by the nations of Eastern Europe, with the USSR reigning supreme. The Women's World Championships were first staged in Chile, in 1953, and Russia has won 5 of the 8 championships played for since. The European Championships began in 1937, in Rome, and the Russians have won 15 of the 17 tournaments staged. Women's basketball was accepted as an Olympic sport in 1976 in Montreal and the Soviets have won both gold medals that have since been at stake.

In the men's game the standard of play and the level of skill and expertise in the USA are far superior to anywhere else in the world; this is not the case in women's basketball. However, since the adoption of the game by American women in preparation for the 1976 Olympics (they had previously played a strange seven-a-side version), their standing has risen dramatically. The world of women's basketball is holding its breath in eager anticipation of the tremendous clash of skills and contrasting styles expected when the USA meets the USSR in Los Angeles in 1984.

OUR NATIONAL TEAMS

England has entered the Women's European Championships, held biennially, since 1966, and, like the men's teams, the girls have to enter a qualification tournament in order to reach the European Finals. In 17 years, four Englishmen have coached the England Senior Women's team: Brian Coleman, Kerry Mumford, John Collins and Roy Birch. Strangely, no women have been involved with the technical preparation of the senior team, although there have been female assistant coaches of junior national teams. And yet, the two nations aspiring for the next Olympic gold medals are coached by women – the USA by Pat Head and the USSR by Lydia Alexeeva.

The record of England's women's teams in European Championships is only 5 wins out of 37 games. In nine attempts England has qualified only once for the Finals. But the achievement of reaching the Finals, in 1980, was a great 'fillip' for English basketball. Over the years there has been tremendous rivalry between the women's

OPPOSITE: *Anita Curtis and Lyn Boenke (Avon) prepare to double team Debbie Miller (Southgate) during the 1983 championship final*

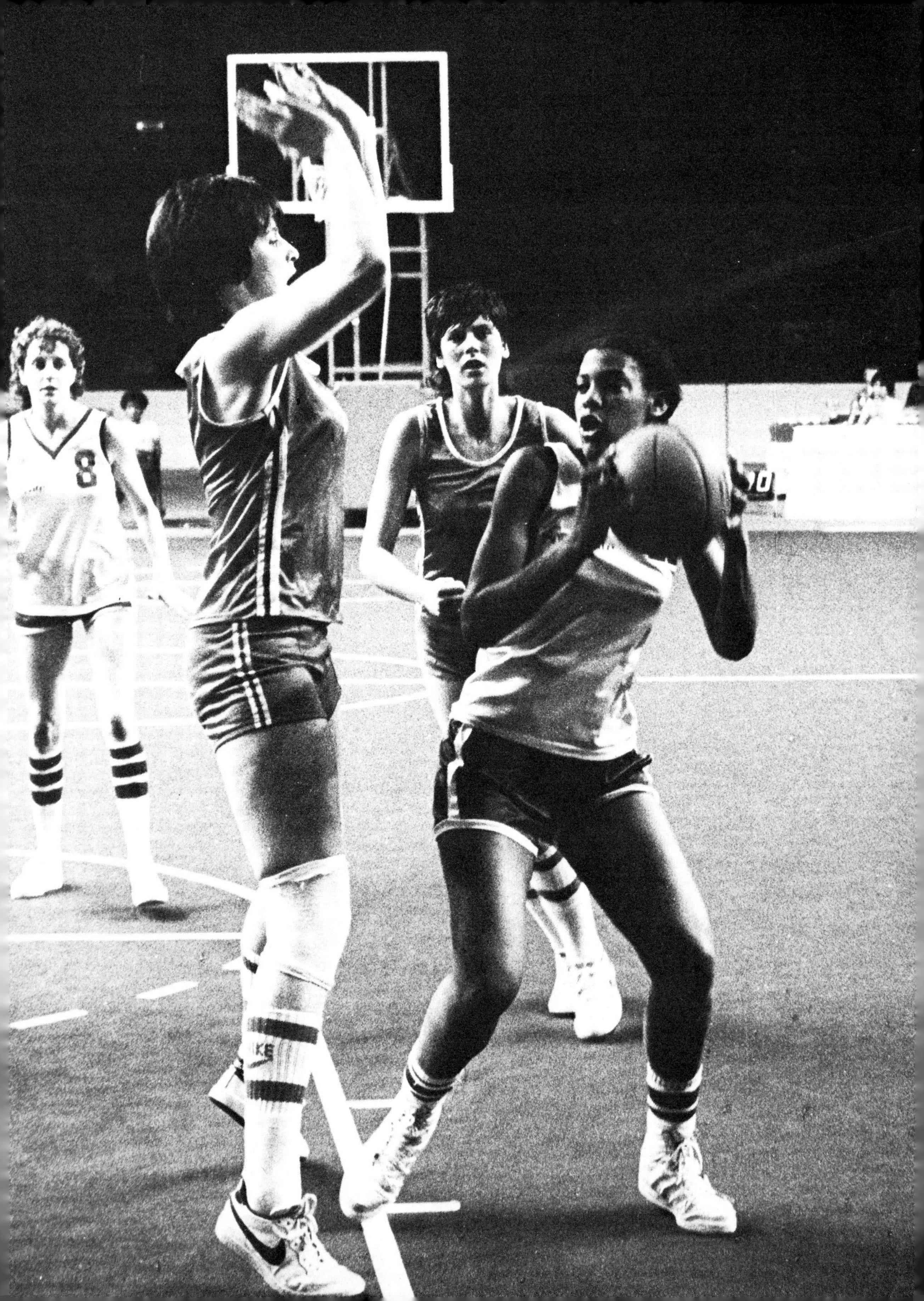
8

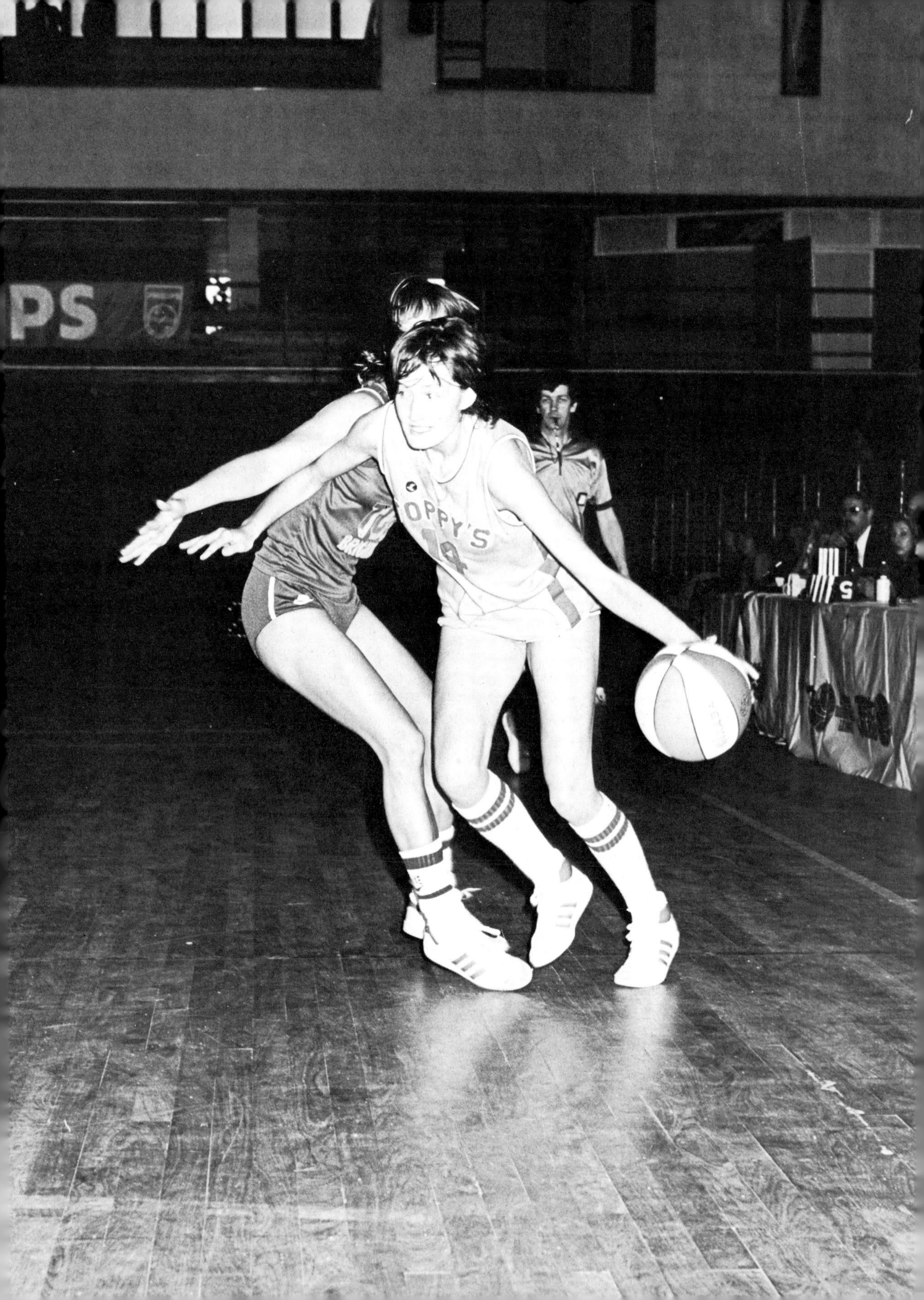

OPPOSITE: *Janice Pope goes to the hoop, displaying the intensity that has won her a four-year basketball scholarship in Indiana*

and the men's teams, with an unofficial contest to see who could be the first to reach the European Finals; the girls beat the guys by twelve months!

England's qualification-winning second place in Vigo, on Spain's Atlantic coast, in April 1980 is a study in dedication and motivation by players and coaches tired of being European 'also-rans'. John Collins (coach) and Roy Birch (assistant coach) put the girls through eighteen months of tough, rugged, sometimes brutal training, as they were conscious of the robust nature of European basketball. Before the four-team tournament in Spain, there were many hard-fought friendly matches, as well as the inaugural British Championships which England won most convincingly. The newspaper headlines that greeted the team in Madrid read: 'Spain sure to qualify - England are on holiday!' In a warm-up game Spain beat England 95-81, and the Spanish fast-break was the decisive factor. The host nation was England's first opposition in the actual qualification tournament, and, before their own TV cameras, they felt less than charitable towards their unfancied rivals: England was soundly thrashed 103-66.

Morale was at a low ebb. But an unexpected Israeli win over West Germany (the other two competing nations) left a glimmer of hope for England. Israel won 64-62 playing on a tide of patriotism against the well-prepared Germans. Collins and Birch were certain that England had the beating of Israel and that qualification was therefore dependent on getting a good result against West Germany. However, England had never got even close to either of their next two opponents; in fact, West Germany had run out 30-point winners only two years previously, and Israel were rated at least twenty points better. Against West Germany the game plan was to keep things close, win or lose, in order to give maximum effort against Israel in going for a big win.

English girls can rarely have entered a sporting arena with such desire or intensity as the ten players who took the floor on two hot nights in April 1980 in Vigo. West Germany led until the last thirty seconds of normal time when Laura Boorman, battered and dazed, stood on the foul line, aware that the game plan had been followed to the letter. She missed both free throws, but the England captain, Anne Gollogly, grabbed the rebound against opponents more than a foot taller than her, and converted to take the game into overtime. The coaches demanded attentiveness, as any loss of concentration could have laid the game plan in ruins; the ultimate aim was still a close result, even in defeat. But the Germans were devastated. That five-minute overtime period was played on pure emotion and England won a famous victory, 64-61. The cost was high, however, as two key forwards, Marian Millen and Pauline Birch, had both picked up painful ankle injuries.

But against Israel, with the winners guaranteed qualification, sheer determination and desire took first place over pain, and Millen and Birch played major roles, scoring 33 points and taking 20 rebounds between them. Anne Gollogly, battling through a very physical Israeli press, scored 18 second-half points, shooting at an amazing 100 per cent. England trounced the stunned Israelis 79-64.

That year, 1980, was the most physically demanding year in the history of international women's basketball: the European qualifying tournaments were followed quickly by the Olympic qualifying tournament in Varna, Bulgaria, then the Olympic Finals in Moscow and, lastly, the European Finals in Banja Luka, Yugoslavia. To take part in three of the four major events of the year meant considerable sacrifices for several English girls. In Varna, England and Scotland combined well as Great Britain and came very close to both the World Championship silver medallists, South Korea (65-78), and the European silver medallists, Yugoslavia (56-64). In fact, a very surprised FIBA official, Dr Ferenc Hepp, estimated that the British girls had been within two turnovers of producing the most astonishing result *ever*, against Yugoslavia. Then Great Britain recorded their first Olympic victory by soundly beating Mexico, 70-55. The

English girls had hardly drawn breath, and it was time to pack their bags for Yugoslavia!

Observers at home, on seeing the results, must have been disappointed with England's fourteenth place, with no wins from seven games. But the fact of the matter was that the team for the Finals was weaker, through injuries, than that which had qualified. Disaster struck in the opening match against Poland when the starting centre, Carol Andrew, broke her ankle; the other centre, Anita Curtis, suffered agonies with a recurring knee problem. Already the smallest team at the event, England were forced to play without a recognised centre for much of the time. However, the results were respectable, notably a one-point overtime defeat by France, a nation which in 1970 had thrashed England by over ninety points!

The outstanding memories of 1980 for the English players and coaches were those thrilling matches in Vigo and Varna, and the long-awaited awesome sight of the mighty Russians, who play what has been described as 'total basketball'.

THE CLUB SCENE

In England women's basketball was first taken seriously in 1965 when the Women's National Cup competition first began. Malory (Lewisham) were the first winners of the National Cup, beating Sheffied Hatters 42-24 in the final; they went on to win the Cup a further three times.

Old photographs of those matches still cause a few smiles, as the national champions, led by the then England captain, Jean Sullivan, played in skirts; modern players would not be seen dead playing in such attire! After Malory, the Abbey Wood club won the Cup three times. And then came the era of Tigers (Hertfordshire) and Eagles (Cleveland), who fought their own north v south battles and almost completely dominated the women's game for the best part of a decade. Eagles appeared in seven finals, winning two, and Tigers played in an amazing eleven finals, winning the National Cup eight times. The Southgate club has since won the Cup twice.

Some of the personalities of the National Cup include: Judy St Ange, a truly remarkable leaper who played as a fourteen-year-old for Malory; Martina Bartanova, a Czechoslovakian refugee playing for Abbey Wood; Annie Brown and Anne Gollogly, both playing for 40 minutes with painful injuries yet emerging worthy winners in 1975; Pauline Birch, playing in 12 finals and scoring at an unequalled 16 points per game; Anita Curtis, taking her teams to four finals but not yet being a member of a Cup-winning side; and the incredible Jacki Wainwright, playing in sixteen national finals, 12 times as a member of the winning team.

The Women's National League began in 1975 and in its eight-year history there have been only three names on the Johnson Matthey trophy: Tigers, Eagles and UDT Southgate. From an original entry of five clubs there are now 25, competing in two divisions. None of the initial five was sponsored, but now 18 of the league's contestants carry a sponsor's name.

Towards the end of the Tigers and Eagles era, 920 screaming fans packed Dacorum Sports Centre, Hemel Hempstead, to see Tigers squeeze Eagles 62-59. That crowd figure remains a record for the women's league. Avon Cosmetics (Northampton) are now the best-supported club with regular crowds of over 500.

Four English women's clubs have participated in European club competitions: Tigers, Eagles, Southgate and Solent. But the European approach to women's sport is vastly different to our own, as Tigers realised when they won through to the second round of the Champions Cup, in 1971, and were drawn against the highly-financed French side, Clermont Ferrand. One of the French girls, Jackie Chazalon, is a sports personality known all over Europe, and has made a career in basketball. Her team was able to train all day, every day, with top-quality coaching and facilities. The teachers, secretaries and housewives playing for Tigers were able to train but once a week. An aggregate score of 299-98 to the French reflected the difference in standards. However, from that 'baptism by fire', English clubs have continued to learn, and in 1979 Tigers battled through to the quarter-finals of the Ronchetti Cup. Both Southgate and Eagles too have successfully despatched Portuguese

Joannie French (Southgate) and Avon's Anita Curtis and Alison Sage (8)

opposition to reach the second round of the Champions Cup.

There is a limit of two foreign players per team in the men's league, but women's clubs are presently allowed only one foreigner. Notable overseas players who have contributed to the development of the game include dual nationals Laura Boorman, Carol Andrew and Candy Ferris (Australians), and Americans Joannie

French, Debbie Miller, Maggie Joseph, Kathy Andrezkowski and Kelly Camp. With the advent of imported talent and sponsorship, the leading clubs are now UDT Southgate, Avon Cosmetics (Northampton), Crystal Palace Toppys, Ashfield Glass (Nottingham), Stockport and Solent.

ABOVE: *Debbie Miller plays high post against Anita Curtis*

OPPOSITE: *Joannie French (14) of Southgate keeps a rebound alive against Janice Pope in a Crystal Palace-Southgate match*

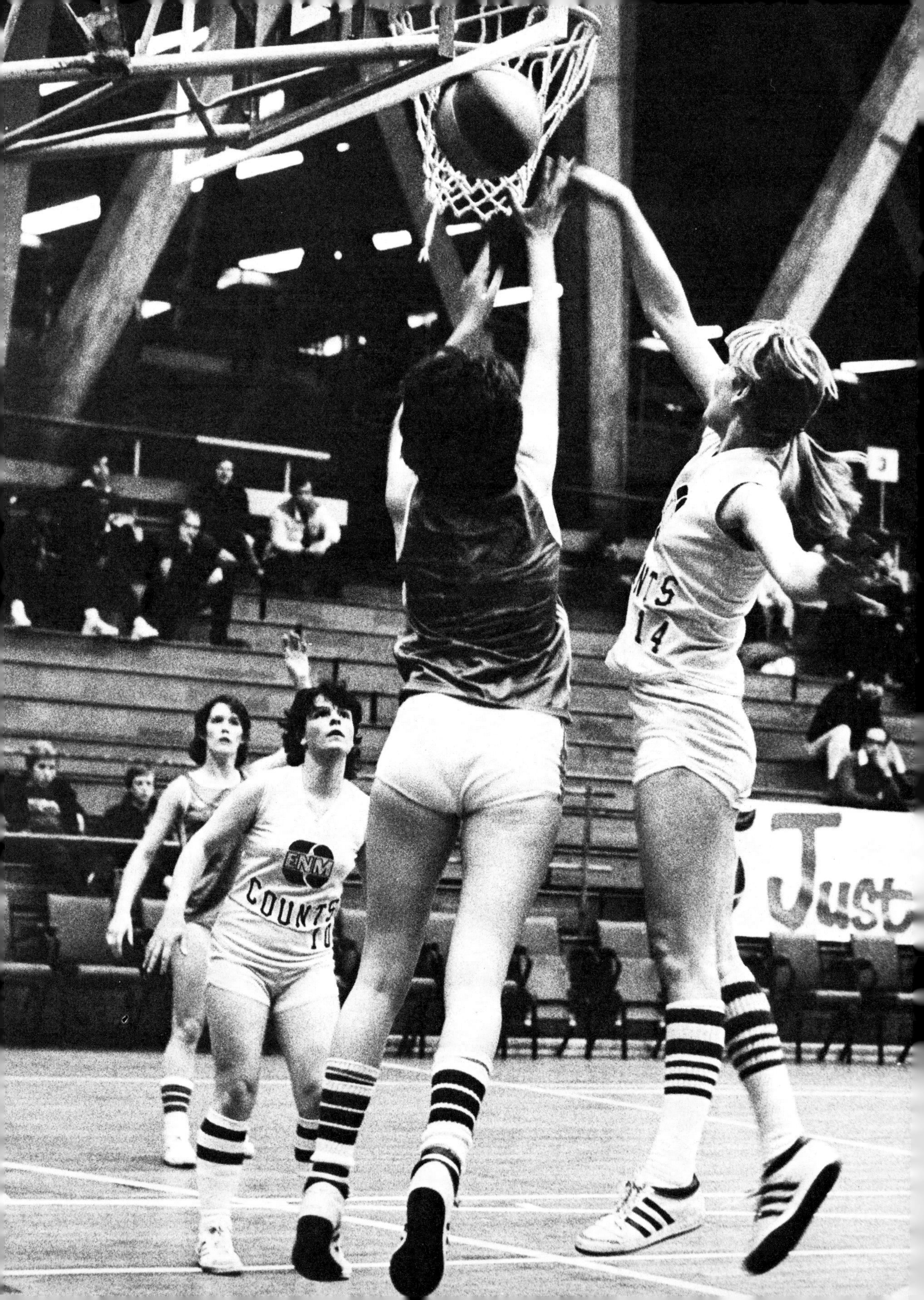
ENM
COUNTS
10
14
Just

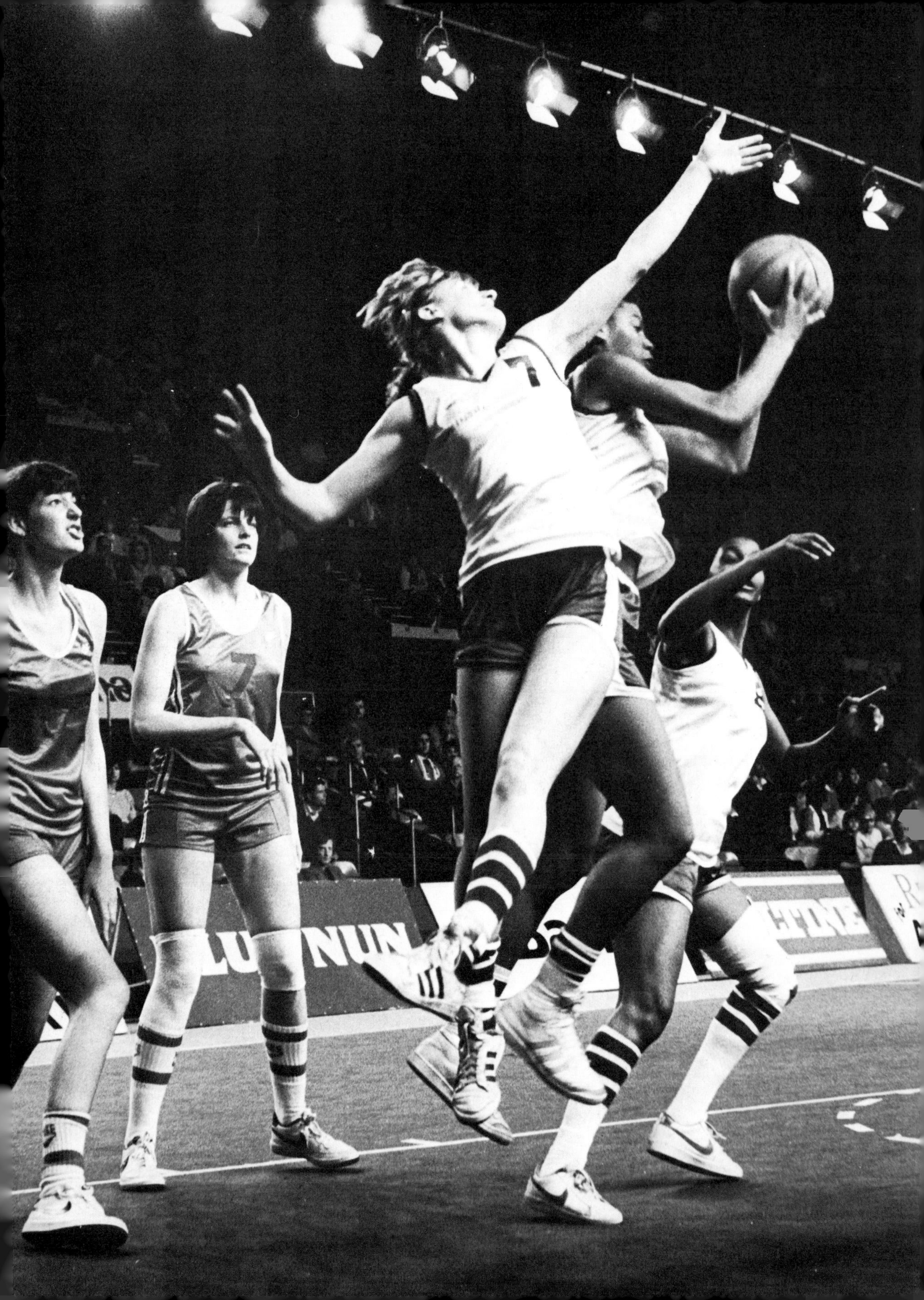

After dominating the game for almost a decade, Eagles and Tigers both withdrew from the league. But Eagles have a new nesting-place in Newcastle and look ready to soar again; and Tigers, far from hibernating in Hoddesdon, Hertfordshire, are rearing some lively cubs!

DEVELOPMENT

Basketball can offer young girls a great deal: it is a healthy and athletic activity which combines competition and aggression with grace and beauty; and it is stimulating to the mind, as well as to the body. Basketball also provides opportunities to meet people and to make many new friends. Three players, Pauline Birch, Anne Gollogly and Jacki Wainwright, have each gained over 60 England caps and have travelled to over 30 different countries. Literally any young girl can play basketball – height and size are not excluding factors. The captain of the Great Britain Olympic team in 1980 is a prime example: as a 15-year-old, Joy Ackland was a 'rotund little thing' (her own words), but she became determined to be a basketball player. She worked hard, got herself into excellent physical condition and learned as much as she could about the technical side of the game; but above all else, she was able to motivate herself to be part of a winning team. Joy's reward has come in the shape of national team and club honours galore, and in being named as England's 'Woman Player of the Year' for two consecutive years, 1980 and 1981.

From the original handful of women playing in the early 1960s, there are now over 8000 registered senior women playing for clubs all over England, and hundreds of thousands more playing in schools. Many have played and then retired to have families: Betty Codona, from Sheffield, played in the 1965 National Cup Final and her two daughters, Vanessa and Lorraine, both play for the present-day Sheffield club and have both played for England Juniors.

The development of women's basketball in England is presently being hampered slightly by two factors: firstly, it is viewed by many as a slow and dull version of the men's game; and secondly, most clubs play in premises which cannot accommodate many spectators. Counter-measures must be taken by coaches and administrators who should study women's basketball around the world. In Europe, the Far East, Australia and the Americas women and girls play attractive styles of basketball and are watched by thousands of fans in purpose-built spectator halls. English coaches must be prepared to employ the fast break in preference to a slow, 'set-play' type of offence, and to use aggressive pressure defences instead of the commonly accepted zones which choke all creative instincts.

OPPOSITE: *Fran Baker (7) and Graclyn Williams (8) with Southgate team-mate Debbie Miller during the 1983 Wembley championship final against Avon*

8 Coaching Skills and Tactics: Ball Handling

INTRODUCTION by Dan Lloyd

This section is not a coaching manual as such but an attempt to help younger players, adult beginners and spectators learn about the fundamentals of the game.

Basketball is first and foremost a team game in which the impact of the whole is far greater than the sum of the individual parts. There is little scope for the 'star' in today's game: there are five individuals on court and the quality of play, both in England and abroad, is such that it will take the pooling of all their talents to win. So all the individual skills I'll be describing, such as passing, dribbling and shooting, should be placed in the framework of team play.

After the skills, I'll be dealing with how they can be put to best effect in the game situations of offence and defence, describing a few basic plays and picking out and comparing the qualities of some leading players. I'll also be revealing some of the tactics which have made my team, Crystal Palace, the most successful in Britain.

BALL HANDLING

Ball handling is the most important facet of the offensive game. The two basic ball-handling skills are passing and dribbling; you can be the greatest shooter in the world but without these skills, you'll seldom get the chance to shoot.

The player who is usually best at both passing and dribbling is the point guard. If you look at any of the top teams in England and Europe such as Crystal Palace and Real Madrid, they all have ball-handling guards with the ability to bring the ball up court, then either drive for the basket for a shot or pass the ball to someone who is in a better position. At Palace we've had Alton Byrd and Dave Shutts in recent seasons and at Real they have Juan Corbalan. They can all pass and dribble *par excellence*. You'll notice in the English league, too, that most of the point guards are Americans. That is because ball handling is, in my opinion, the weakest part of the English player's game. In America you get used to ball handling from an early age in the way you learn to kick a football! here. Give an American a football to kick and he'll look very clumsy, but give him a basketball and he'll show you all sorts of tricks!

DRIBBLING

Ways to improve your dribbling

Crouch low to the ground and try bouncing the ball first round your right leg a few times and then round your left leg. Do it clockwise five or six times and then anti-clockwise.

After that, try doing the drill in a figure-of-eight pattern through your legs. Remember, keep your knees slightly bent and your head up. Try to get the feel of what you're doing without looking at the ball all the time. In a game situation you'll be looking around to see who's free to pass to and whether an opponent is about to try to steal the ball.

- Use only the flat of your fingers and the outside of your palms. You *never* use the full palms of your hands for anything in basketball, not for shooting, passing or dribbling.
- Don't slap at the ball. Use the fingers, wrist and lower arm. Some people use the whole arm, going up and down with the ball; this won't give them any control. Dribbling should involve a fluid wrist motion, just following through waiting for the ball to come back up again like it was a yo-yo. This way you'll get maximum control.
- Keep the ball as low as possible, ideally between knee and waist, so as to make a 'steal' more difficult.

COACHING SKILLS AND TACTICS: BALL HANDLING 79

Dan Lloyd demonstrates his figure-of-eight routine to improve dribbling skills

Pete Jeremich practises his ball handling by dribbling two balls at once, one for each hand

The speed dribble

There are two basic dribbles: the speed dribble and the controlled dribble.

The speed dribble is used in an open-court situation where you have a clear run to the basket and want to advance the ball as quickly as possible.

Keep the ball a step-and-a-half in front of you, on the right side if you're dribbling right-handed and on the left if you're dribbling left-handed. Never let the ball get level or behind you because it will either slow you up or allow an opponent to sneak in for a steal.

It's important to practise both the left-handed and right-handed dribble. The ability to use both hands in basketball is as important as the soccer player's ability to use both feet, if not more so. Any good defence will quickly manoeuvre the one-handed player into a position where he is forced to switch to his weaker hand, thereby making a steal more likely.

Since the emphasis is on speed, you can afford to bounce the ball higher and stand more erect. Remember to try not to look at the ball too much. The object in a game situation is to watch for a team-mate running into a shooting position or for a shooting opportunity yourself.

To improve your two-handed ability, try practising with two balls at once, one for the right hand and one for the left.

The controlled dribble

When you get nearer the basket, the emphasis changes from speed to control. Opponents will be closing in and you're going to make it difficult for them to intercept.

- Slow down
- Crouch low to the ground
- Keep the bounce as low as possible
- Keep your body between the ball and your opponent for maximum protection.

With the controlled dribble, you're looking either to go by your opponent or to pass the ball. If you try to go by it will have to be to his left or right. The crouching position will help here to move in either direction quickly.

OPPOSITE: *T. J. Robinson and the dribble in action*

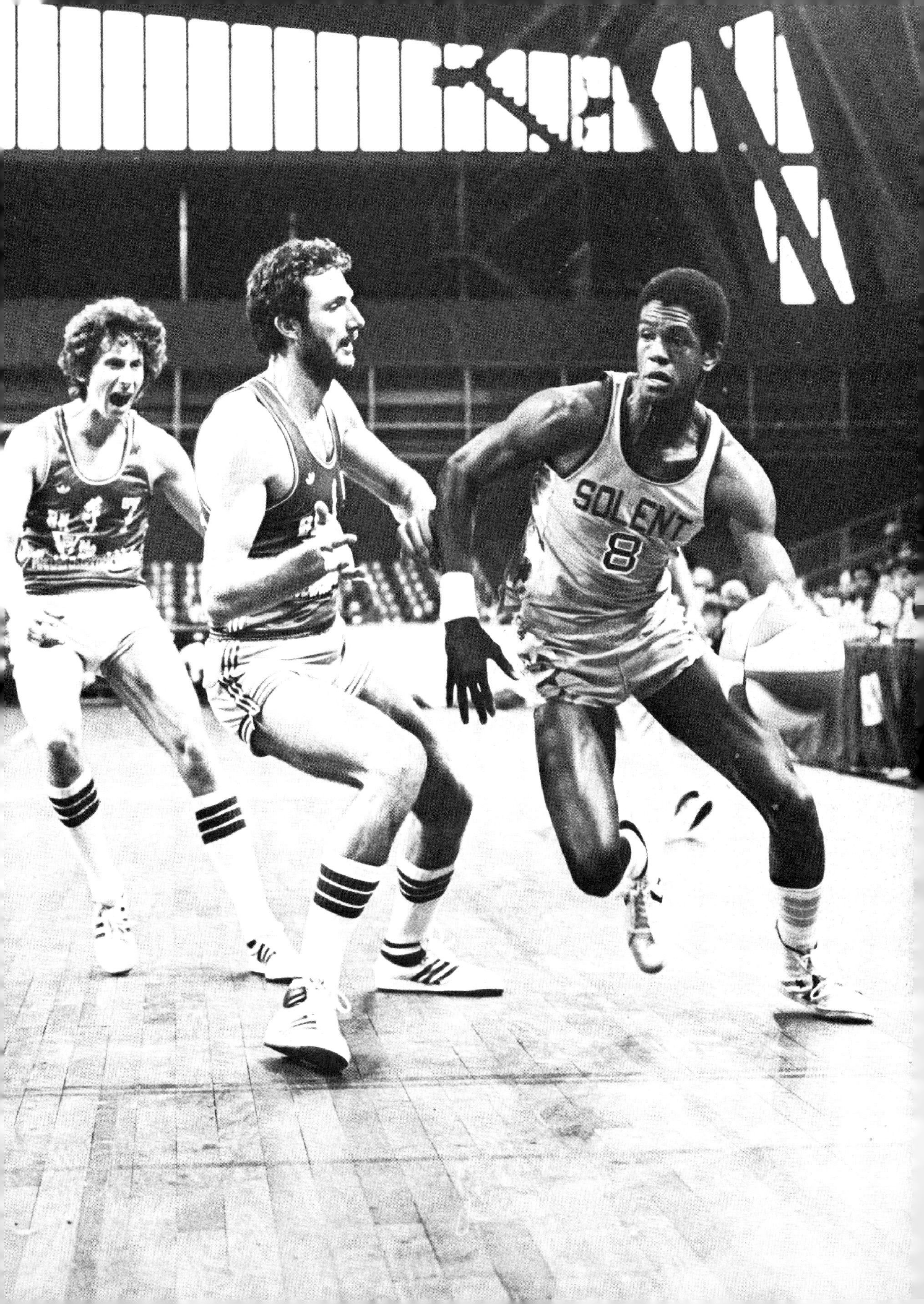
SOLENT
8
7

TOP ROW: *Dan Lloyd practises the fake with Joe White: moving to go left, switching right, and leaving his man wrong-footed*

BOTTOM ROW: *Dan Lloyd demonstrates the chest pass*

I'd like to introduce here the art of the fake. It's like selling someone a dummy in soccer. You act as though to go one way and then go to the other. The fake is a fundamental ploy in basketball and it should be practised in every situation, in both dribbling, passing and sometimes in shooting. In each case the object is to deceive your opponent for long enough to enable you to go by him, make a telling pass or take a shot.

In both the above dribbles, try incorporating fakes to left and right by switching from one hand to the other.

PASSING

If it comes to a choice between passing and dribbling, coaches would always want their players to pass the ball. The reason is simple: you can move a ball up court far more quickly by passing than dribbling. Seconds count more in basketball than in almost any other ball game and the quicker you are, the more chance you stand of succeeding. The other even more important reason for passing is that basketball is a team game and the best way to beat your opponents is by using all five players on court. That requires accuracy and smart thinking. You have to be able to pass the ball to the right place at the right time.

Solent's Karl Tatham is a good example of a player who can penetrate a defence and then lay off a perfect pass, often with a fake shot thrown in to deceive his marker. It's a pleasure to play with people like that because they make your job so much easier. Once you see a player driving to the basket you should look for an open avenue yourself, get in a good scoring position and wait for the pass. What distinguishes the great passer from the good passer is that the former will give you the ball at precisely the right moment, as you're going to the basket and before an opponent has time to cover.

There are three basic passes: the chest pass, the bounce pass and the overhead pass.

The *chest* and *bounce* passes use the same technique. Place the hands either side of the ball, again use fingers and outside of the palms only, and keep the thumbs pointing up and fingers forward.

Draw the ball into your chest keeping your elbows in, then flick the ball away using your wrists and lower arms. Your thumbs should follow through in a downward motion and as your elbows come out, the action should finish with your palms facing out and your thumbs down.

Always take a step forward when you pass. This will give your pass extra momentum.

The *chest* pass is a short-range pass made chest to chest when there is minimal danger of an opponent making an interception. The *bounce* pass is for when you want to bypass an opponent by bouncing the ball under his hands.

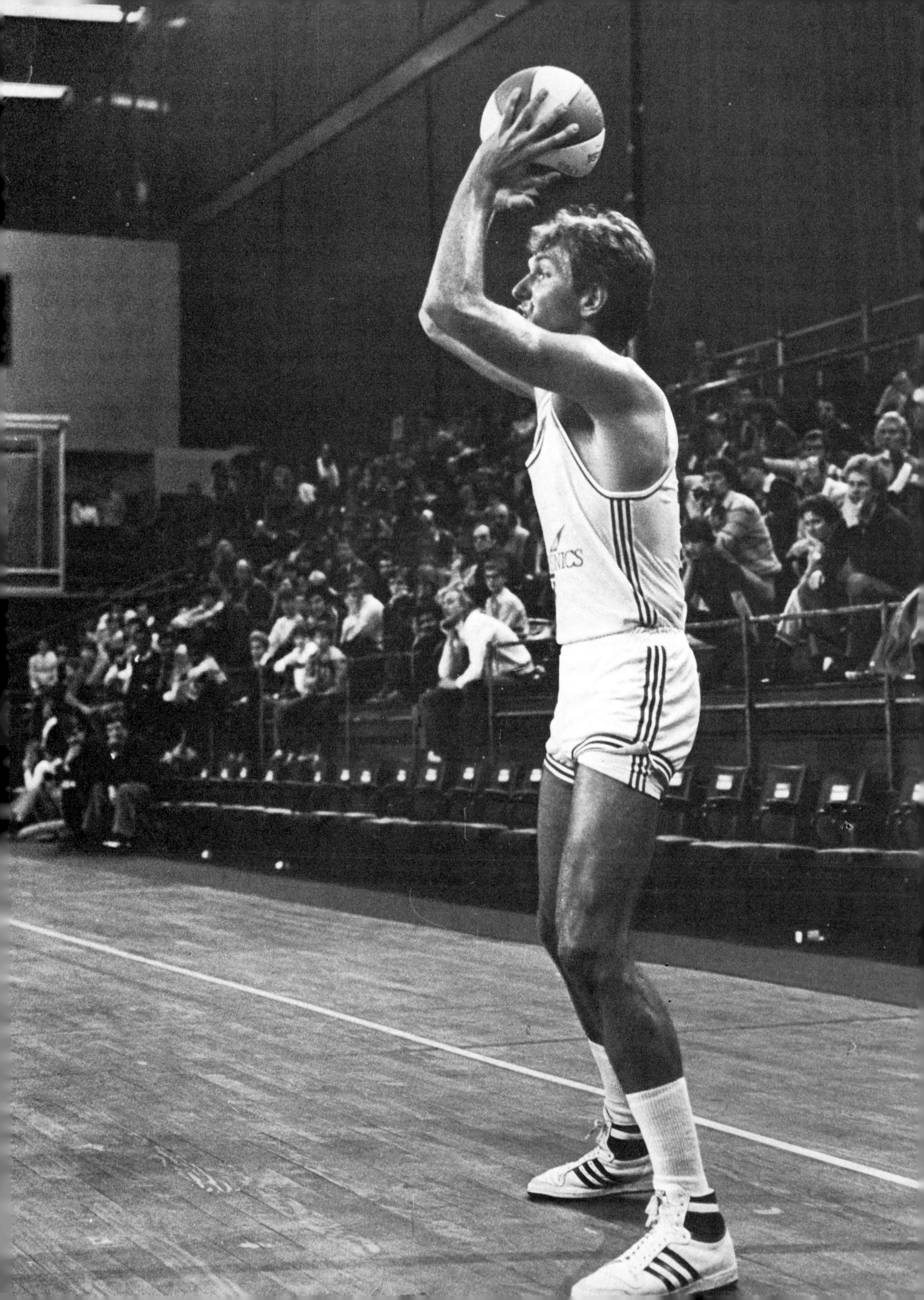

COACHING SKILLS AND TACTICS: BALL HANDLING

In this case the ball should bounce about halfway or two thirds of the way to the person you're passing to, so that it rises up for a comfortable catch. The last thing a player wants when he is in a good scoring position is a pass around his ankles. Waist-high is fine for a bounce pass.

When you are trying to bypass an opponent, either under his arms with a bounce pass or over them with a chest pass, remember to aim as near his body as possible. By his shoulders and either side of his chest are the points where he will find it most difficult to intercept.

The third sort of pass, the two-handed *overhead* pass, is the type you see at a throw-in at soccer. The difference is that the ball doesn't go behind the head because this invites someone to grab it away. The grasp is the same as for the chest pass but this time the ball travels head-high or higher. This is a pass frequently used by rebounders because they need to get the ball away as quickly as possible to prevent the risk of a steal.

The overhead pass is also a good way of starting a fast break, where you want to get the ball up court before your opponents have time to regroup. In this situation it's called an *outlet* pass because it provides the outlet which sets the offence in motion. I'll go into the fast break in more detail in the next chapter.

One other type of pass frequently seen is the *baseball* or *javelin* pass. This is a one-handed pass you see goalkeepers make in soccer sometimes. It's more difficult than the others because you need a big strong hand to control the ball, but it's useful for achieving distance. A rebounder who's under pressure and needs to get the ball as far away from the opposition as possible may use a javelin pass. Players will also use it when they want to throw the ball the length of the court, say to a player who is in a good scoring position.

Other passes not seen so often but which can be useful in certain situations are the *through-the-legs* pass, the *behind-the-back* pass and the one-handed *hook* pass round an opponent.

OPPOSITE: *Pete Jeremich with the two-handed overhead pass*

Of the various passes I've described, the chest, bounce and two-handed overhead types are the ones I'd recommend younger players and beginners to concentrate on. Using two hands will help give good direction and ball control, while the one-handed pass is more for older, more experienced players.

Passing drills

If you're practising on your own, mark a spot on a wall about chest-high, go back about four or five feet and aim chest passes at that spot. Try it for 10 or 15 passes, throwing, catching, throwing until you work up a rhythm.

To work on your quickness and coordination, try doing it with two balls. This is a type of horizontal juggling where you're throwing one ball and immediately catching the other.

If you're working in groups, you can practise passing by playing pig-in-the-middle. One person stands in the middle of a circle of players who try to pass to each other without the one in the middle being able to intercept. This is also an ideal situation in which to practise faking. You fake to pass in one direction, wrong-foot the player in the middle and then pass in another direction. You could fake with a chest pass then make a bounce pass.

All the while the object is to keep the defensive player – the one in the middle – on his guard. If there are enough of you, you could practise with two players in the middle. This will be more like a game situation when you're trying to pass the ball 'in traffic' – that is, with defenders all around you.

SHOOTING

Shooting is the end result of all offensive moves. What you're working for is a good shot. Some teams will have players they rely on to shoot but they're not usually the teams who win many prizes. The winning teams have players who are all good shooters. As well as being, in that respect, the most important aspect of the game, shooting is also the easiest to practise. All you need is a ball and a basket – and even they are not essential if you're a beginner. One of the best shooters is my pal Pete Jeremich, and he learned his shooting by aiming tennis balls into a coffee

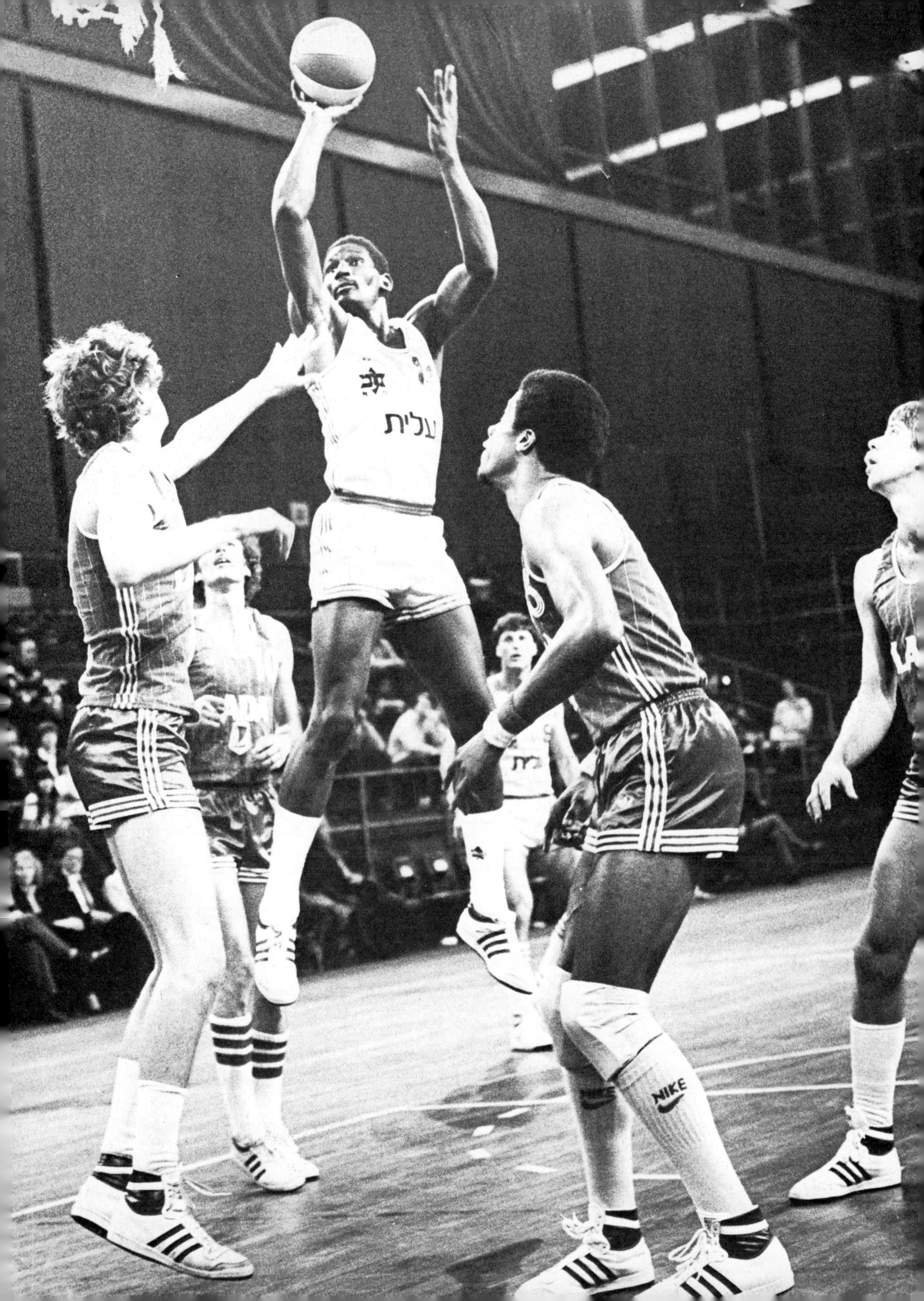
עלית
NIKE

ABOVE: *John Johnson shows the triple threat position – ready to dribble, pass or shoot.*

THE TRIPLE THREAT: *Once you have received the ball, the best way to keep your options open is the 'triple threat' position. It enables you either to pass, dribble or shoot and, most importantly, doesn't tell your opponent what you intend.*

Crouch as in the shooting position, keep the ball chest-high and close to the body, with elbows out and feet spread. You are now ready for action.

OPPOSITE: *Earl Williams in elegant shooting action for Maccabi against Warrington in the Philips Tournament at Crystal Palace in 1983*

can he'd opened at both ends and hooked up on the bedroom wall.

In game situations and when you're practising with a basketball, it's essential to have your whole body facing the basket. Your feet, knees, hips, shoulders and head should be square when you shoot.

There are three basic shots: the lay-up, the jump shot and the free throw, and they all require the same technique.

Your body weight should be on the balls of your feet, your knees slightly bent and your body slightly crouched as though it were a spring ready to recoil. Your hands should be in the triple-threat position, your right hand (if you're right-handed) behind the ball slightly cocked back and your left hand on the side of the ball.

The shooting action is like a spring action. Your body recoils up, you launch the ball from around your forehead and your hands follow through. The follow-through is very important because it provides the final touch which will govern the accuracy of the shot. You should feel the ball coming off your index finger and your middle finger. The strength of the shot comes not from the arms or the shoulders but from the legs. The other point about shooting is that the left hand is for steadying the ball only, it plays no part in the shot. Remember also that the palms of your hands shouldn't touch the ball, only your fingers and the outside of the palms. Finally, keep your head up and your eyes on the basket.

The lay-up

The easiest shot in basketball is the lay-up. This is a relaxed shot from right under the basket when there is no pressure. It's the shot you'll see players make when they're unmarked and have a clear run. They go right up to the basket, take a good jump and lay the ball in off the backboard.

If you're coming in from the right-hand side, you should be jumping off your left foot about two or three feet from the basket and aiming your shot at the top right-hand corner of the square marked on the backboard. The reverse applies if you're left-handed, although as with dribbling, it's important to be equally proficient with both hands. There will be situations when you have to approach the basket from the left side and you'll need to use your left hand.

Lay-up drill A good way to practise the lay-up using both left and right hands is the George Mikan drill in which you jump off your left foot and shoot with your right hand, catch the ball, take a step, jump up off your right foot and shoot with your left. This is a particularly good drill for getting your footwork right.

The jump shot

This is more of a distance shot which you make either because your path to the basket is blocked or because you're under pressure either from an opponent or because time is running out. My Crystal Palace team-mate Trevor Anderson took one of the most crucial jump shots of the 1982-83 season in our television match at Birmingham. He was 30 feet out with two seconds left on the clock when he took the shot that sent the game into overtime. That's about the maximum distance even top-level players would try with a jump shot. This type of shot covers any field goal that's further out than a lay-up, but the most usual distance is between five and 15 feet. You'll often see it when a defence is marking areas of the court rather than individuals (a zone defence), so making it harder to get near the basket.

As with the lay-up, you start coiled up and then jump straight up in the air. Don't try to jump forward because you may run into an opponent and commit a charging foul. Similarly, don't fall away from your shot because that could make it fall short of the basket.

When you jump your whole body should be coiled up. Release the ball only when you're at the top of your jump. In that action your whole body should straighten out, with your arms simultaneously straightening out in the direction of the basket.

The rest of the action is the same as for a lay-up, except that you're not aiming for the backboard but for the ring itself. Don't aim in the general direction of the basket but go for the centre of the ring itself. Remember also to flight your shot with a nice arc. Some players, like Jim Brandon of Sunderland, have a very flat trajectory on their shots but that calls for even greater accuracy than an arced shot.

Jump shot drill A good way to practise the jump shot is to work in a game situation. Dribble to the left of the basket, stop, pivot, face the basket, jump and shoot. Now try driving to the right of the basket. Dribble with your left hand if you're going to the left of the basket and with your right if you're going right. That way you will always be shielding the ball from your inside marker with your body.

Start with shots close in and gradually work your way back to get a greater range.

Maccabi's Micky Berkowitz goes for the lay-up

Dave Shutts executes the perfect jump shot

Dan Lloyd jump shooting

Dan Lloyd demonstrates the free-throw routine: bounce, coil and recoil

The free throw

Although it's supposed to be one of the easier shots in basketball, the free throw doesn't always work out that way. The reason many players miss is because the shots are taken out of the game situation. You can momentarily lose concentration and perhaps also your rhythm.

The action of the free throw is the same as for a lay-up and jump shot except that your feet don't leave the ground. You should relax and feel comfortable, bring the ball up slowly, and throw. You should complete the action standing on tip-toe and again I'd like to stress the importance of the follow-through. The other characteristic of the free throw is that it should follow the same pattern every time. Whereas you may have to vary the jump shot now and again depending on the circumstances, the free throw should remain the same. In that way you'll soon learn to feel comfortable and get into a rhythm of throwing. Most players bounce the ball on the floor a few times before each shot so that they work up a rhythm.

The hook shot

You don't see this too often but it's a useful shot to have in your repertoire, especially for the taller player. Unlike the other shots I've described, this one is made when you can't face the basket. It's a shot made sideways and close to the basket with the ball brought up with the hand furthest from the basket and looped or hooked over the head. The advantage for the tall player is that it is a very difficult shot to block.

The player who made this type of shot famous in the United States is Kareem Abdul Jabbar of the Los Angeles Lakers. He's around 7ft 4in and he could bring the ball over and down from such a height that it was called the 'sky hook'. But there is no reason why much shorter players shouldn't attempt it, especially when they are confronted by taller players. As I've said, it's a difficult shot to block because the arm is coming down from quite a height, and in certain situations that can be more advantageous than a jump shot which taller players may sometimes find easier to block.

REBOUNDING

A rebound is any missed shot that hits the backboard or the rim of the basket.

One of basketball's favourite sayings is that the team that collects most rebounds wins the game. The theory behind this is that for every ten shots a team takes, only five or six will succeed. That means four or five opportunities for both sides to gain, or regain, possession. So the team that can take most rebounds is going to have more opportunities to score and therefore win.

It's self-evident that if the defending team can take the rebound they're limiting their opponents to just one shot per possession. The opposing team will therefore be forced to shoot a very high percentage to win the game.

Positioning is more important in rebounding than jumping ability. Mark Saiers of Solent is one of the best defensive rebounders in the game, not only because he's a big, strong player but because he positions himself well. Notice how he gets between the basket and the player he's marking to prevent him getting to the ball first. This is called 'boxing out' and in any top game you'll see the defending team boxing out their opponents. They'll be crouched facing the basket, feet and arms spread to prevent the offensive player breaking through.

Rebounding is as much a team effort as any other aspect of the game. It's no use one player boxing out if his team-mates are leaving other areas open. Defending players should form a triangle round the basket, about four or five feet out, to cover where the ball may fall.

Good rebounding teams will have their mar-

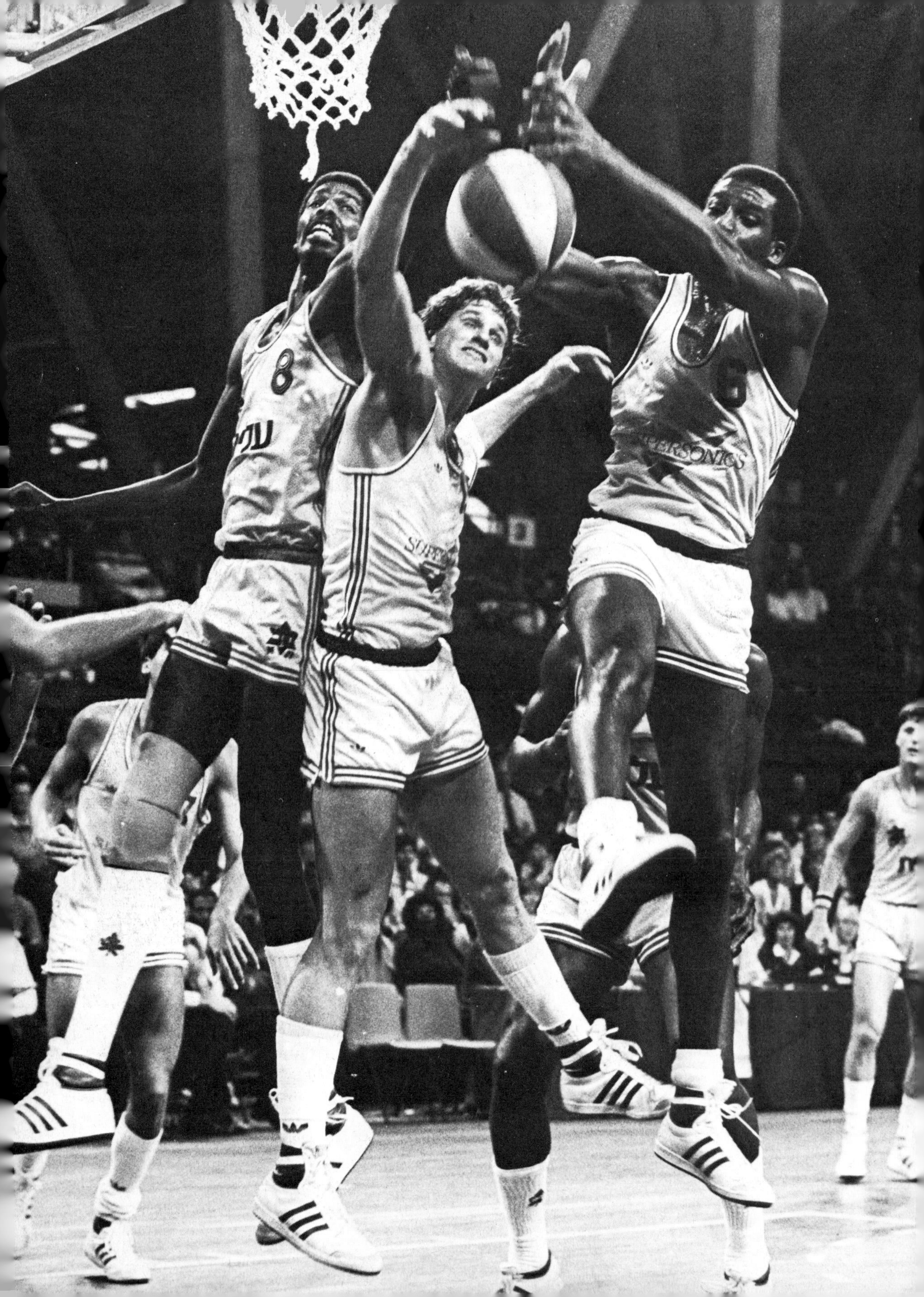
SUPERSONICS

ABOVE: *Mark Saiers (10) has his man boxed out as Paul Philp shoots*

OPPOSITE: *Battle of the boards: Dan Lloyd and Greg McCray (right) beat Maccabi's Aulcie Perry for the rebound*

kers so far boxed out that no matter how good the markers are at jumping, they won't get near the ball. Although basketball is supposed to be a non-contact sport, this is one of the areas where there has to be contact. You box out your man by physically preventing him getting near the basket.

When jumping for the ball, good timing is essential. Try to reach the ball at the top of your jump, not before or after. Use both hands and

Ken Kocher (10) of Sunderland battles for the rebound with Pete Jeremich during a league match at Crystal Palace

hang on tight. Having gained possession, look for the outlet pass – the two-handed overhead pass or the one-handed javelin pass which will set up a fast break. Crystal Palace use this method a great deal, as I'll be describing later, but teams like Sunderland and Hemel Hempstead, who rely more on set plays, will often let their rebounders bring the ball up court.

9 The Offensive Game and the Defensive Game

THE OFFENSIVE GAME

Basketball involves two separate games which are played simultaneously. The team in possession of the ball will go on the attack – called the offence – and the team without the ball will defend and try to recover the ball without conceding a point. To be a good all-round player, it is essential to be able to play both offence and defence equally well.

The offensive game involves doing everything to help your team score points, whether it be passing, dribbling, shooting or rebounding. But it also involves more than these skills: moving without the ball and getting into a scoring position is equally important. You cannot expect to be able to stand in one position and wait for a pass. You have to keep on the move and try to give defenders the slip for long enough to take a pass and make a shot, or grab a rebound.

One player who is good at this aspect of the game is my brother David. He's not an intimidating player and he's not that quick or fast, but he's a smart player in that he's always looking for scoring opportunities. You won't see him dribble or drive to the basket when he's in possession, but when he doesn't have the ball defenders tend to forget about him. The next thing they know is that he's under the basket for a lay-up.

Having a player like that is very useful because he'll force the opposition to mark him more closely and so take the pressure off other players. Many players don't pay this part of their game as much attention as they should and their overall play suffers as a result. They tend to get in the way of their team-mates and disrupt the rhythm of the offence.

Ken Kocher of Sunderland goes for the jump shot against Birmingham

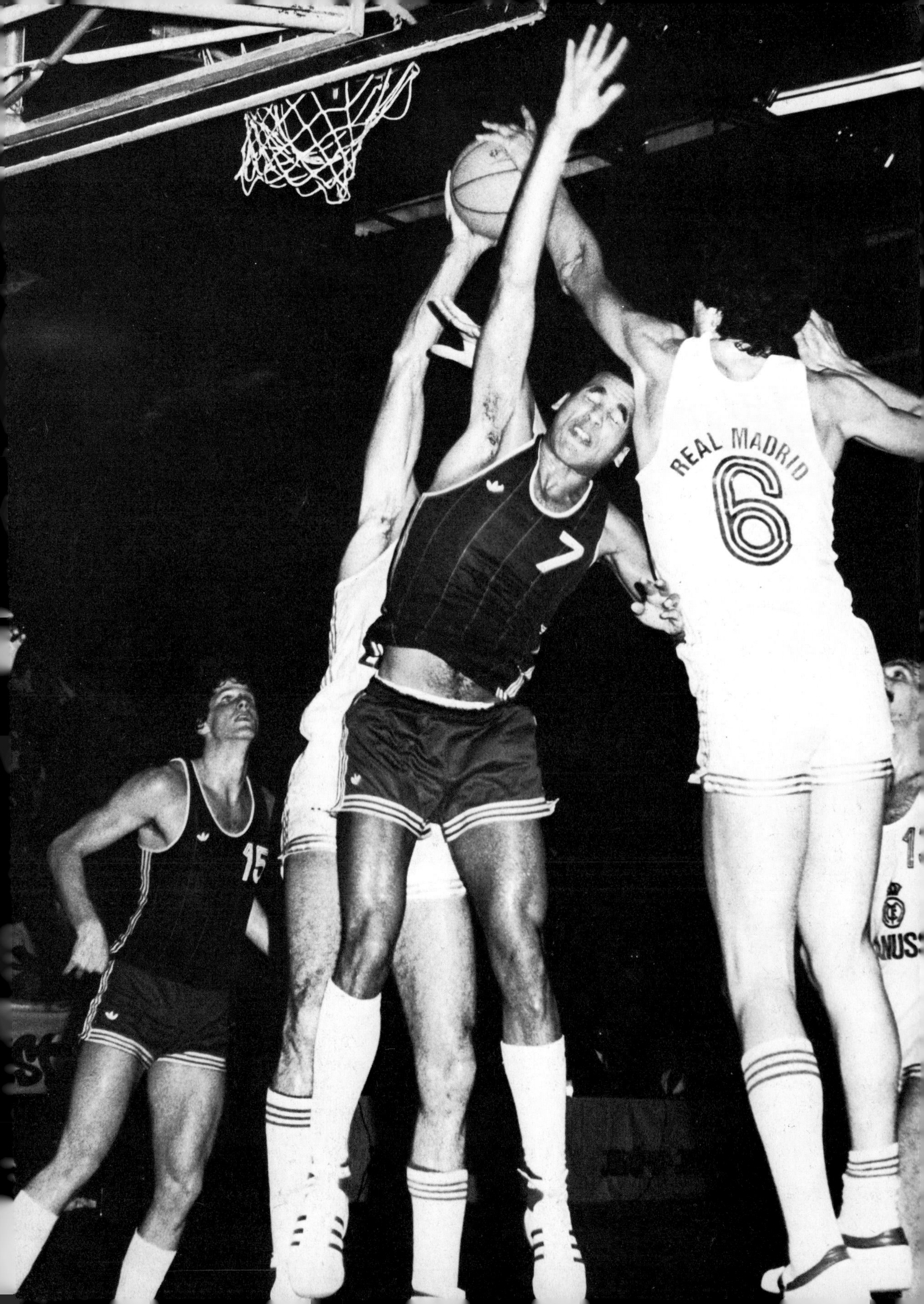
REAL MADRID
6
7
15

OPPOSITE: *Crystal Palace's John Johnson is squeezed out going for an offensive rebound against Real Madrid*

Before attempting any of the basic plays I'm about to describe, remember these important points:
• The first thing you do when you receive the ball is turn and face the basket. You won't accomplish anything in offence unless you're facing the basket in the first place, If you like, it's the Mecca of your play
• Put the ball in the triple-threat position so you have the option to shoot, pass or dribble.

The simplest team moves in offence are *give and go*, *pick and roll*, *backdoor* and the *fast break*. In each case the object is to free one player for a good scoring opportunity.

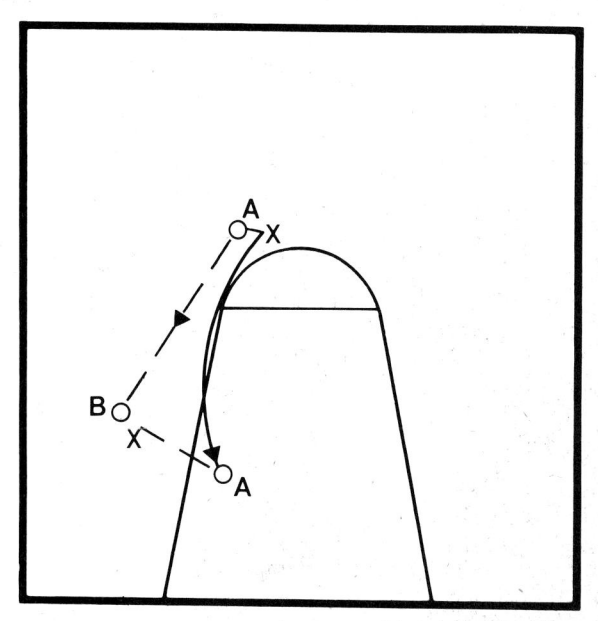

GIVE AND GO

This is the equivalent of soccer's one-two where you make a pass, run for the basket and look for a return pass. It's frequently made between a guard and a forward. The guard will pass out to the wing, fake to move to the opposite wing in order to wrong-foot his marker and then cut towards the basket for the return pass. Another variation is when a forward passes the ball from the wing inside to a centre who then fakes and cuts to the basket for a shot.

Notice that each of these moves is set up with the fake. As I've already said, it's an integral part of offence and should be incorporated into every individual's first move with the ball.

Give and go is used on most areas of the court and is used at every level of the game. Many coaches depend on it for the majority of their team's points.

PICK AND ROLL

This is another coach's favourite. Here an offensive player picks or screens (that is, he blocks) a defender in order to release a team-mate or himself for a scoring chance.

It works like this. The player with the ball passes out to the wing, fakes to move to the other wing and then cuts across to pick the marker of the player he has just passed to. This

Give and go
A passes to B, then fakes left and cuts to basket looking for a return pass

X defensive player
O offensive player
— — — pass
———— cut

allows the player with the ball to fake as if to move outside and then cut inside the pick. As soon as the defending player makes contact with the pick in his attempt to stay with the man in possession, the pick should pivot round and roll for the basket.

One of two things can happen next. If the defending player goes with the pick, the man in possession will be free for a run to the basket. If the defending player goes to cover the man in possession, the pick is free to take a pass and go for the basket.

Two important points to remember with pick and roll are that the pick should always be facing the man with the ball so that he knows what's going to happen next; and when the pick rolls for the basket, he should always have the hand furthest from his marker up in the air ready to receive a pass. That way there is less danger of an interception.

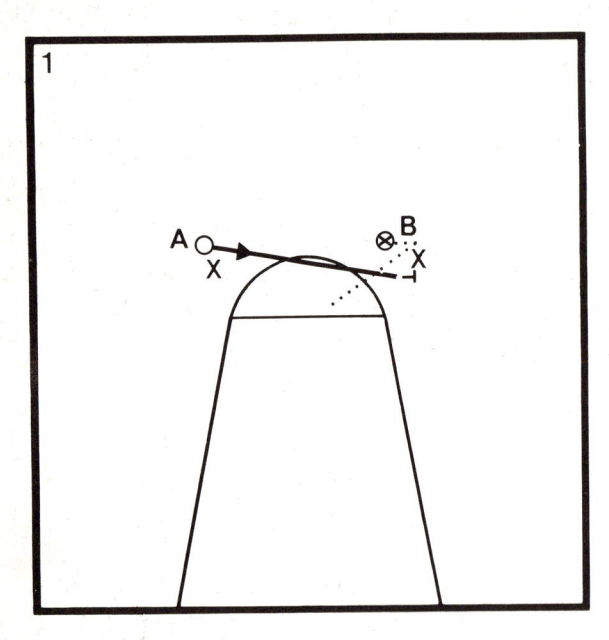

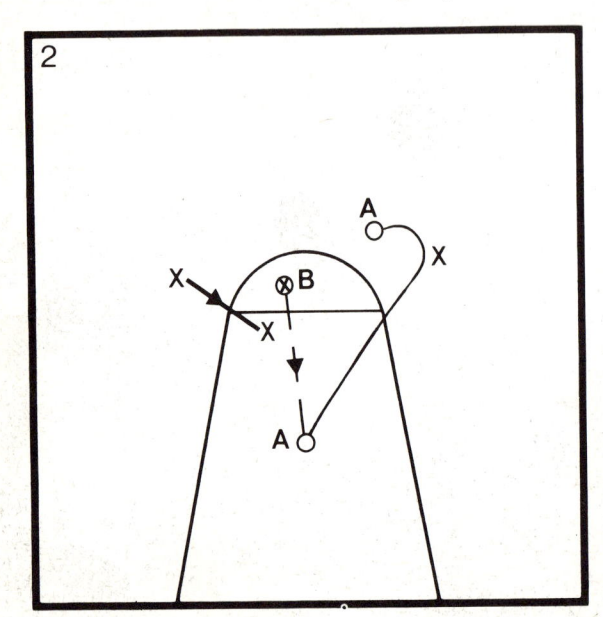

Give and go and pick and roll are basically two-man moves but they can also involve three men and will often be more effective for doing so. You have five players in a side and the more you can utilise the better. In a three-man pick and roll, for example, you pass one way and then set a screen on a player on the opposite side of the court. That frees another team-mate to go for the basket and take the pass.

BACKDOOR

This is a move designed to free a player not in possession but who is being marked so tightly that he cannot be brought into the game. Here the player, who is usually on the wing, will run towards the team-mate in possession, then cut back towards the basket at a sharp angle in order to 'throw' his marker. He's then free to take the pass and go for his shot.

OPPOSITE: *Maccabi's Micky Berkowitz demonstrates his dribbling skills against Solent*

BELOW: **Backdoor**
B's man is preventing him receiving the ball from A by 'overplaying' him, so B cuts away from basket, stops and cuts back to throw off his marker and get into scoring position ready for a pass from A

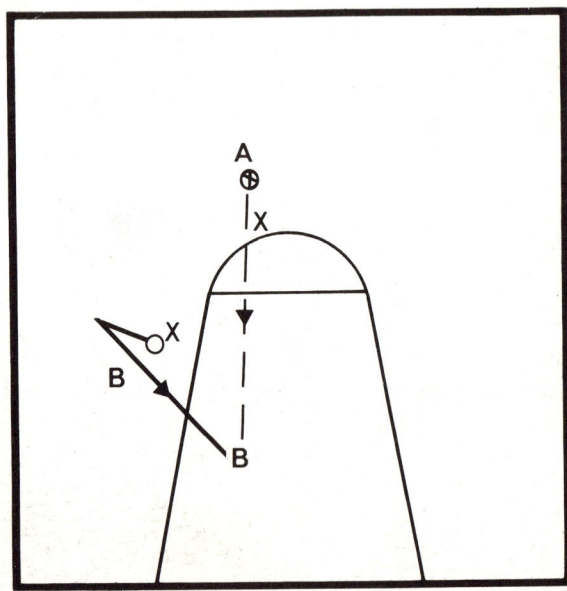

Pick and roll
1. A sets a screen on B's man, B then fakes left and dribbles right towards basket 2. A then has B's man on his back as he pivots and rolls to the basket, looking for a return pass from B

X   defensive player
O   offensive player
⊗   offensive player with ball
— — —   pass
⋯⋯⋯⋯   dribble
───────   cut
⊣   pick/screen

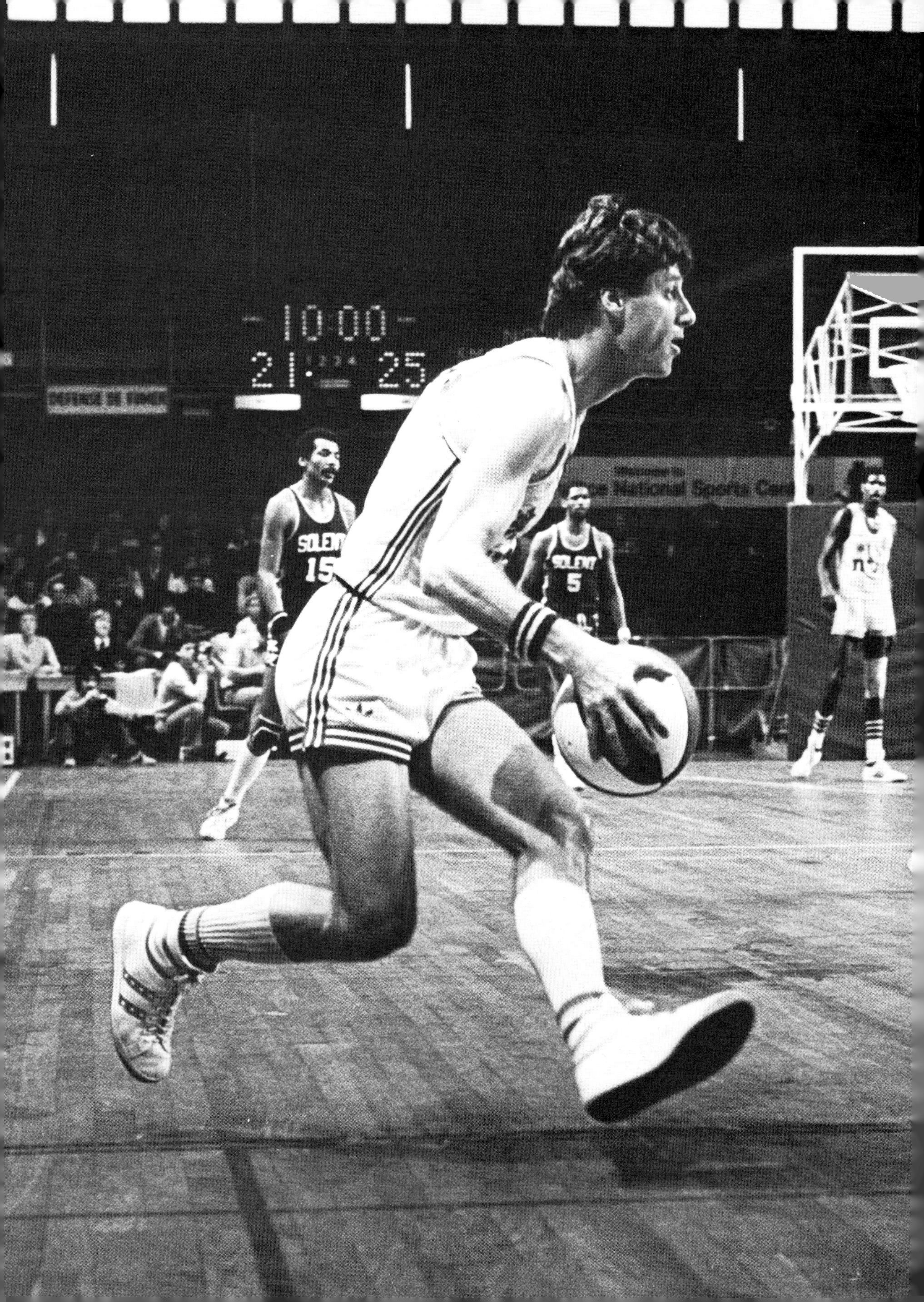

10:00
21 25
SOLENT
15
SOLENT
5
National Sports Centre

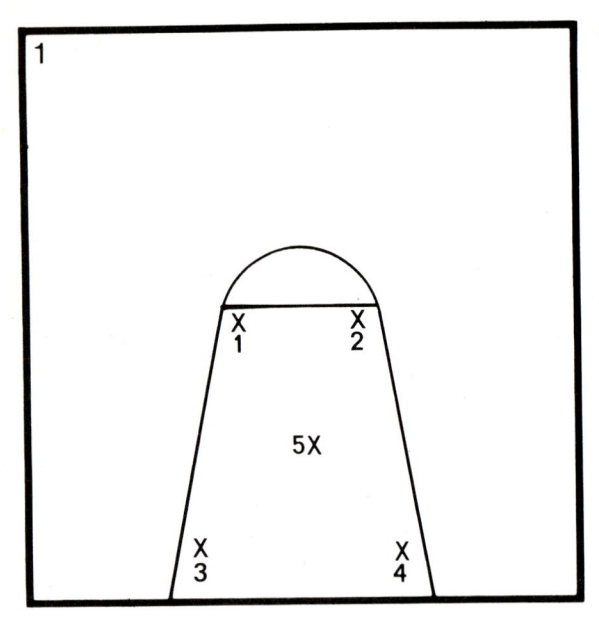

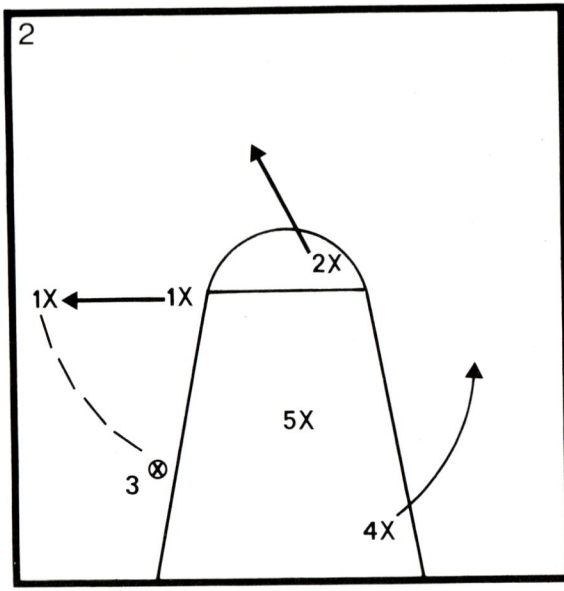

Outlet and fast break

1. Defending players form rebounding triangle with guards 1x and 2x in position for a long rebound
2. Whichever side the ball goes to, that guard breaks into the outside edge of court in line with free throw line, looking for outlet pass
3. Guard 1x, having received ball from forward 3x, for example, passes on to other guard, 2x, in mid-court. Forward 4x breaks on opposite 'weak' side of court looking for long pass from either 1x or 2x
4. End result is either a lay-up for players 1x or 4x or an easy jump shot for 1x, 2x or 4x

X defensive player
O offensive player
⊗ offensive player with ball
— — — dribble
· · · · · · · · pass
——————— cut

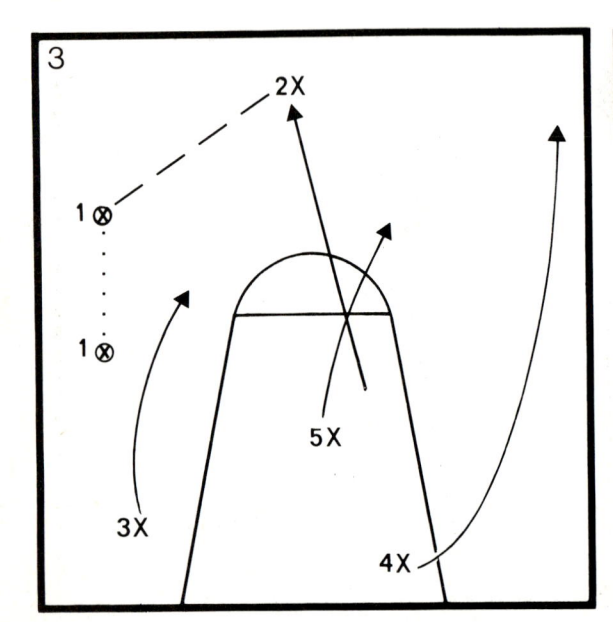

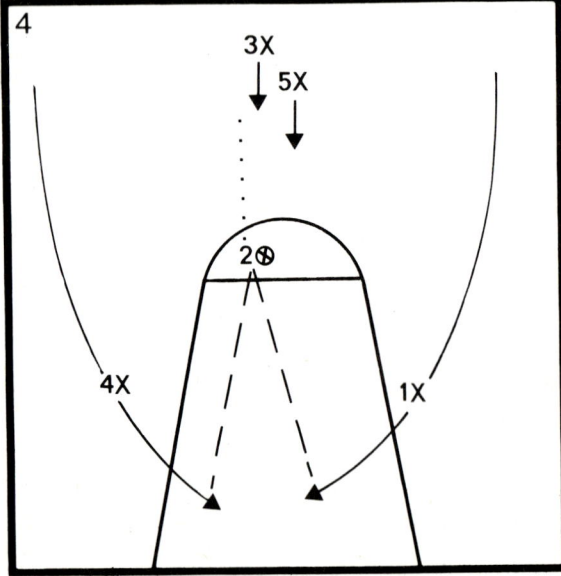

THE FAST BREAK

This is not so much an offensive move as a transition between defence and offence. The fast break should lead directly to an easy scoring chance or it may lead to one of the set plays I've already described. However, its primary object is to establish a numerical advantage over the defence and, as the name suggests, this can only be achieved by moving the ball as quickly as possible.

The fast break is set up with a defensive rebound followed by an outlet pass to the wing. As I've already described, this is usually by means of a two-handed overhead pass which bypasses the defenders and sets up the receiver for a long pass up court. One of your guards, usually your ball handler because he's quick, is the player waiting to take that long pass. He'll be in the centre of the court and he should have at the most one defender to beat. With a teammate in support, he'll either go for a lay-up or pass out to set up an easy jump shot. If the defenders have time to regroup, the fast break will move into a set play.

All the various plays I've described are intended to produce scoring chances as close to the basket as possible. Outside or long-range shots are an important part of the game, but no team can survive on them throughout because players will tire and lose their accuracy.

THE DEFENSIVE GAME

Most people look on defence as the least exciting and glamorous part of the game. But ask any coach and he'll tell you that it's the part which more often than not determines whether a team wins or loses.

I've already dealt with rebounding as a vital element of both offence and defence, so here I'll be covering more general aspects of defence. Unfortunately, these don't often appeal to young players but they have to be learned and practised by anyone wanting to become a good all-round player. It's important to emphasise them at an early age so that playing good defence is taken for granted and not regarded as a chore. Besides, I believe that good defensive play, especially round the basket, can be as exciting as a good offence.

There are two types of defence in basketball:

Palace's secondary fast break (see also p. 110)
1. Players 1, 2 and 3 set up the primary fast break, with 2 and 3 crossing under the basket

2. Players 4 and 5 are the second wave, taking up positions either side of basket ready for a pass from 1

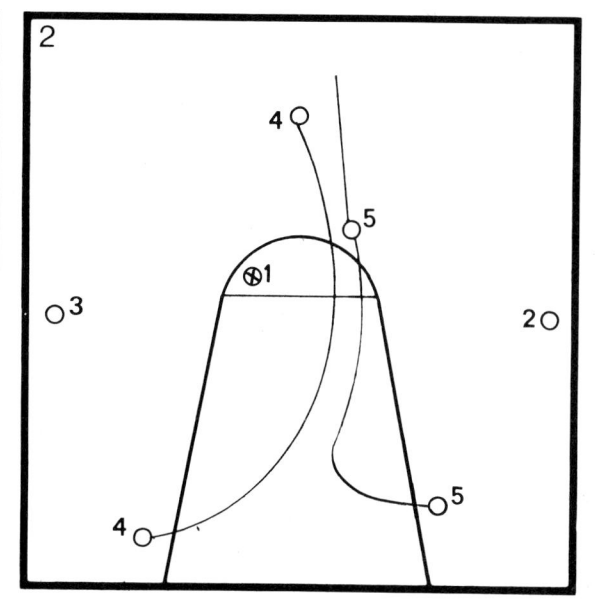

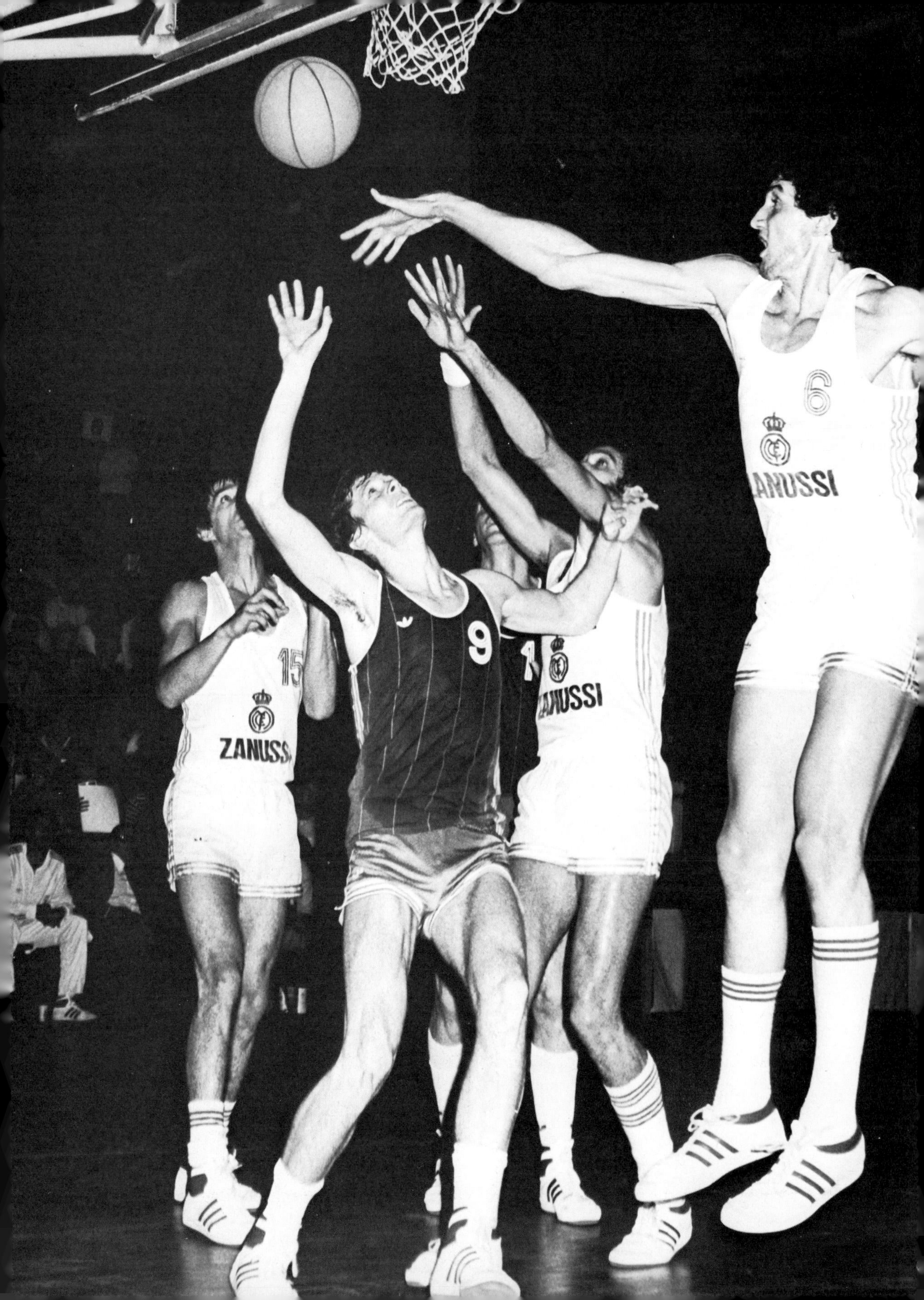
6
ZANUSSI
9
15
ZANUSSI
ZANUSSI

OPPOSITE: *Battle under the boards between Real Madrid's Fernando Ròmay (6) and Crystal Palace's Mick Bett*

man-to-man and zone. Each involves trying to prevent the offensive player from setting up a scoring chance.

MAN-TO-MAN

This is the type of defence usually taught to beginners because the techniques used for both are similar and also because it is easier to teach.

Whereas there are many different zone formations, man-to-man marking can be broken down into two situations: on the ball and away from the ball. In both, the defensive player shadows his opposite number in an attempt to shut him out of the game, prevent him passing or shooting, or to force a steal or turnover.

Before going into these situations further, it's important to develop good defensive technique.

Defence on the ball
Stay between man with ball and basket
X defensive player
⊗ offensive player with ball

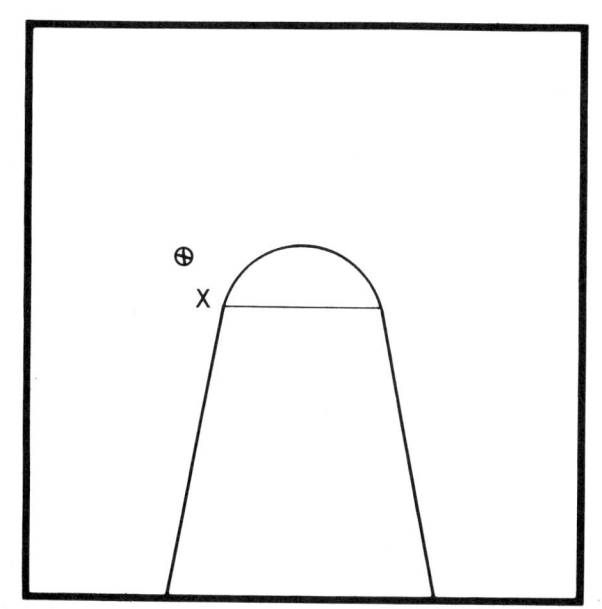

Defensive technique
Stance Adopt a crouching position with the head up and the back straight at an angle of 45 degrees to the floor. Stagger your stance so that the foot closest to the middle of the court is slightly forward. Keep your hands up to anticipate where the ball might go.

Footwork Maintain the stance while moving by means of sliding your feet. Try to stay opposite the middle of your opponent's body, not too much to either side. Play defence by moving the feet while not allowing the hands to reach in too far.

A good team drill to practise stance is the zig-zag. Split into partners, one offensive, one defensive. Starting from the endline, the offensive player dribbles the full length of the court in a zig-zag pattern with the defending player sliding along and staying in front of him.

On the ball One basic rule common to both 'on the ball' and 'away from the ball' situations is that the defender should always be between his man and the basket. But this is particularly important when your opponent has the ball. By staying between him and the basket you are denying him the quickest and easiest route to score. However, to play even better man-to-man defence, you should go one stage further: the defensive player should 'act', thereby forcing the offensive player to 'react'.

The defender should be the aggressor, always forcing the offence to do what is expected. For example, the defending player could position himself slightly to one side, thereby inviting the offensive player to dribble in the direction left open to him. Preferably this should be the side that forces him to use his weaker dribbling hand, thus opening up the chance of a steal.

If the offensive player does decide to shoot, the defender should be in a position to get his hand up in front of the shooter's face. He should not attempt to block the shot unless he is sure he can because fouling the shooter only ends in shots from the free-throw line.

Now and again a player will risk fouling his man if he believes that player may miss his free

The defensive stance

shots. Sunderland's Jimmy Brandon did just that in the 1983 Wembley finals when he fouled Hemel Hempstead's Cedric Frederick rather than risk Frederick scoring a match-winning field goal. Brandon had seen a nervous Frederick miss a couple of earlier free shots. This time he missed all three and Sunderland sneaked into the final.

Away from the ball Here your position in relation to the man you are marking will vary, depending on how close you are to the player with the ball. But one rule you must always follow is to see both your man and the ball.

You can do this by using your peripheral vision and positioning yourself in a defensive triangle of which you are the apex.

By following this rule it is much easier to anticipate where your man will go and to react to his movement. A good defensive stance here is to have your hands up, one pointing to the ball and the other to your man. This will keep you on balance and help your concentration.

Defence away from the ball
Form a defensive triangle so you are in a position to see both your man and the ball
X defensive player
O offensive player
⊗ offensive player with ball

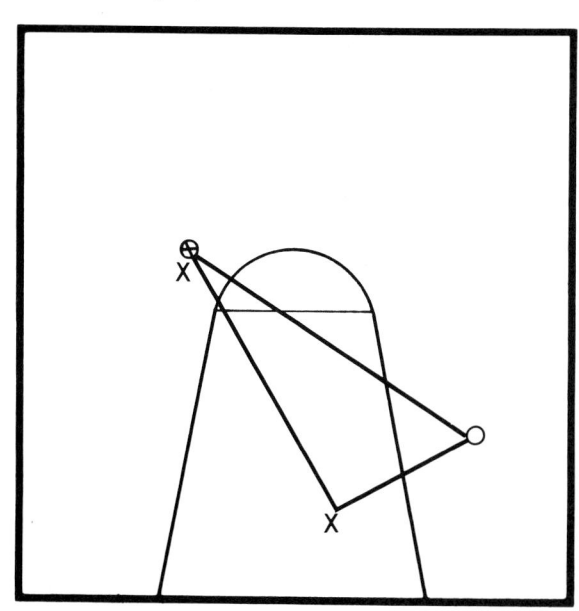

Defensive stance shown here by former Palace player James Clabon

The further you are from the man with the ball, the further you will be from the man you are marking. As your man moves closer to the ball, you move closer to your man; this will keep the pressure on him.

The main objective when playing defence away from the ball is to make it as difficult as possible for your man to receive the ball.

If the only way your man can receive a pass is by going well back from the basket, you will have done a good job. His chances of scoring will be that much less and you will be in an advantageous position when you resume 'on the ball' defence. Also, you will be in a better position to help out if the man with the ball gets past his defender.

ZONE

In this form of defence players mark certain areas of the court rather than marking individual opponents. When an opponent enters that area, he is marked man-to-man in the way I've outlined. It should go without saying that when the ball enters that area, it is the defending player's job to try to retrieve it.

The advantages of zone defence are that it is not as tiring as man-to-man because you're not moving about so much; it can be used when key players are in foul trouble because they can lay back a bit more and not have to worry about contact; and it can be used to force teams to shoot further from the basket.

The most common zones are the 2–3, the 3–2 and the 2–1–2 formations shown in the diagrams.

Harvey Knuckles (Ovaltine Hemel Hempstead) and Sunderland's Jim Brandon (13) ready for any mistakes from the free-throw line

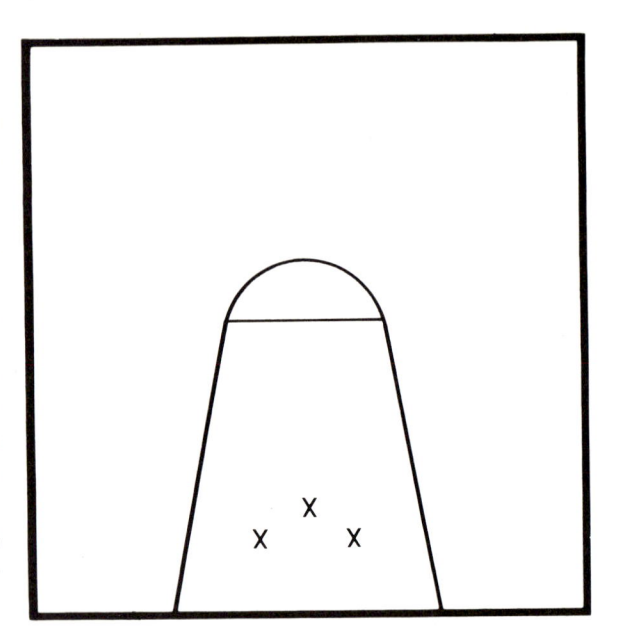

Rebounding triangle
Defensive players have all angles covered for rebound, keeping offensive players as far away as possible from basket
X *defensive player*

In the 2–3 your three best rebounders are round the basket and your two other players in front of them. You'd use a 2–3 against poor outside shooters because it would force them to shoot from outside.

In a 3–2 the formation is the other way round. Here you would be forcing a team of good outside shooters even further from the basket.

The 2–1–2 zone is used against teams who have good inside players because it stops opponents getting the ball to their big men in the middle.

Birmingham showed how a zone could be put to telling use in the league match against Solent which clinched their place in the 1983 Wembley championships. They were eight points ahead when they switched to a zone with some five minutes remaining. It forced Solent to pass the ball round looking for an opening and because of the pressure on them to close the gap, they hurried their shots and lost the match.

Well-disciplined teams will always have the patience to find their way through a zone, but it

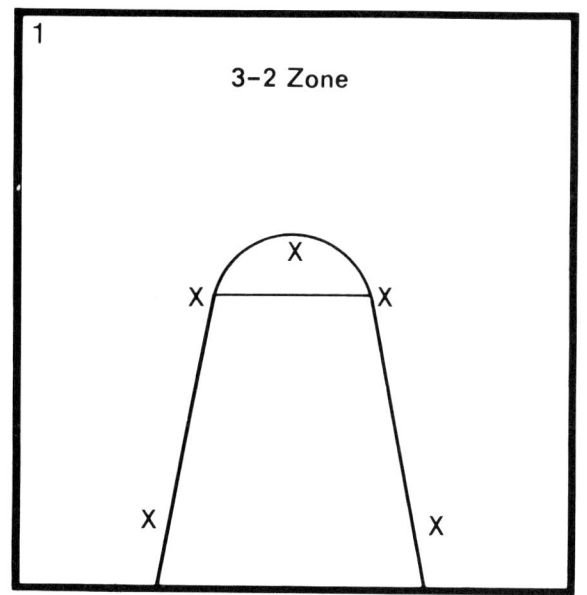

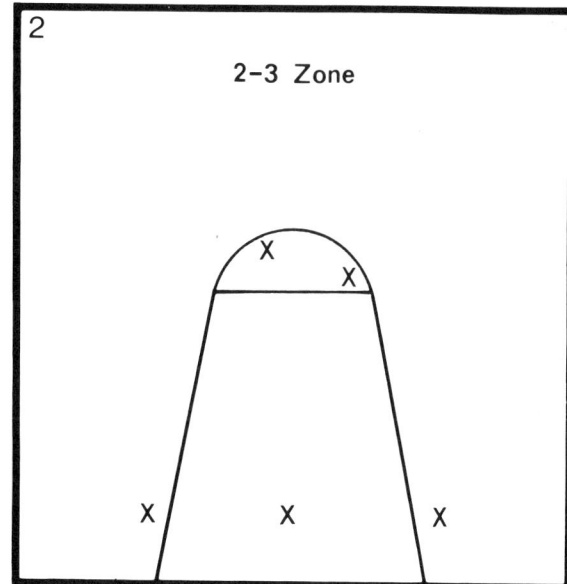

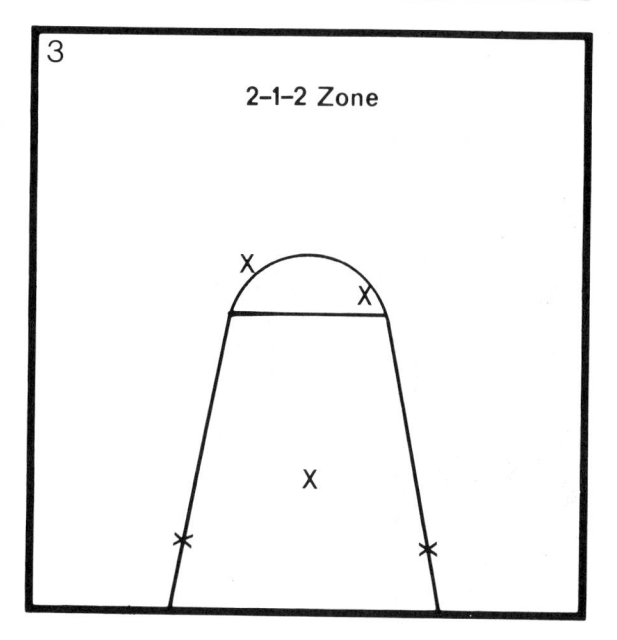

THE OFFENSIVE GAME AND THE DEFENSIVE GAME 109

1
3-2 Zone

2
2-3 Zone

3
2-1-2 Zone

Zone formations

nevertheless remains an effective way of slowing the game down and pressuring teams into hasty shots.

THE PRESS

This is a defensive tactic which can have a number of objectives: to force a turnover; to force a violation of the ten- or thirty-second rules; or to generally unsettle the opposition and prevent them moving the ball around.

'Press' is short for pressure defence and is a very aggressive tactic applied by throwing a cordon of players around the man with the ball. If, for example, you're one point down with only seconds remaining, you would apply the press to try to gain possession. If you're one point up, you would apply it to prevent your opponents getting into a scoring position. As a game tactic, the press should always contain an element of surprise to catch opponents off their guard. Applied over the full court it is very tiring and not a tactic which can be applied very often unless you have good bench strength and are not afraid to do a lot of substituting.

10 Better Play the Palace Way

One of the main reasons for Crystal Palace's reign as Britain's top team for the past decade has been the club's ability to play a style which suits the players rather than making the players suit a style.

As a small team, certainly since I've been here, we've had to play a running game and rely on our quickness rather than our height. We've been well served in that respect by two point guards, first Alton Byrd and then Dave Shutts, who were brought from the United States with the specific purpose of running a fast offence. They can both bring the ball up court very quickly and the running game is very much part of their own style.

Defensively, we've also relied on the full-court press, again because of our lack of height. We like to pressure teams in order to draw their bigger men away from our basket to help break the press. That upsets the opposition's game because obviously their bigger men want to receive the ball near our basket, where they pose the biggest threat. They don't want to have to come looking for it.

In that way we've always managed to dictate the pattern of the game rather then have other teams dictate it for us.

Domestically, we've had the best defensive team in the league for several years and much of that has been due to the efforts of our coach, Danny Palmer, in tightening up that department of our game.

Offensively, we've used a variation of the fast break to score many of our points. This again stems from our lack of height and therefore a big reliance on jump-shooting. At 6ft 7ins Pete Jeremich has been our tallest player – and also about the best jump shooter in the league.

As I described in an earlier section, the fast break relies on one player bringing the ball up court quickly and setting up a simple scoring chance for himself or a team-mate. However, if the fast break fails most teams would have to revert to a set play in order to score. At Crystal Palace we play what we call a secondary fast break designed to make such a failure less likely.

Our point guard brings the ball up court and two wing players complement the move, finally crossing under the basket. But it's the two players trailing them – the second wave of the fast break – who get ready to receive the ball. The guard sets up to the left or right of the free-throw line, the first trailer comes down looking for a pass and then the second trailer. Because the defensive team haven't had time to pick up the men they're supposed to be marking, one of the trailers should be free to make an open jump shot from about 12 feet (see p. 103).

The unselfishness of our players has a big part to play here: we operate very well as a team and we're always looking for each other. If somebody else is in a better scoring position, we won't hesitate to give him the ball because we want the best shot possible.

In defence we use a lot of combinations of zone and man-to-man marking systems. The object is to keep the opposition guessing what we're doing rather than concentrating on their own game. This works in our favour because they're uncertain of the positions they want to be in offensively and they're wasting their 30 seconds shooting time.

OPPOSITE: *Sunderland's Art Wearren tries in vain to stop this left-handed score by Palace's Greg McCray*

8
NDERLAND
ASKETBALL CLUB
6
CRYSTAL PALACE
CEANDA
ADVERTISIN

Palace's Trevor Anderson stretches to beat Sunderland's Clive Hartley to the rebound

Dan Lloyd in action during Palace's historic win over Real Madrid

Substitution has also played a major role since Danny Palmer arrived. He has set an example for the rest of English basketball by showing that substitutes can be used to good effect, even in the tightest situations. Trevor Anderson proved that by saving our skins in a league match I referred to in the section on shooting. Our full-court game also demands constant use of substitutes because it's so tiring. But, more than that using your bench strength gives everyone valuable experience, keeps them involved and keeps them happy. It's good for bringing on our younger players, like Trevor Anderson and Joel Moore, and it's good for team spirit.

Maybe we've made a lot of games closer than they should have been, and perhaps even lost one or two, by substitution, but in the long run our policy will be seen to be successful because of the good young players it will help develop.

If I had to pick one game in which we got our whole act together – teamwork, defence and offence – it would have to be our home leg victory over Real Madrid in the European Cup quarter-final in 1982. Not only was that a milestone in the history of the club, it was also a triumph for everything we'd been working to achieve that season.

Losing Alton Byrd left a big hole in our side

and everyone knew they would have to work harder to fill the gap. In the past there had been a tendency to let Alton go it alone and say: 'Yeah, Alton won that one for us.' When he went we didn't have any individual players who could take the game on their own. It was a case of everybody helping each other. Against Real Madrid everyone performed their team role *par excellence*. They're a team who play fast-break so our basic game plan was to press them full-court and play a lot of zone defence to prevent the ball getting to their big men near the basket.

They're a much taller side than ourselves but Greg McCray was in superb rebounding form, and on offence John Johnson gave one of the best performances I've ever seen. I don't think Real Madrid had often encountered anyone of his inside skill because he was able to get by his man and score almost at will with runs to the basket and baseline drives. He scored 32 points which is a remarkable achievement against a team like that.

Although everyone was delighted we won, I got the feeling one or two fans thought Real Madrid couldn't have been at their best that night. But that takes the credit away from our performance; they weren't at their best because we didn't allow them to be.

11 Who Is the Greatest—Byrd or Saunders?

Alton Byrd and Russ Saunders are living proof that you don't always have to be tall to make it.

Byrd was voted the best American college player under 6 ft before bringing his exciting talent to Crystal Palace in 1979. He was twice voted the NBL's Most Valuable Player in three seasons here, helping Palace achieve their unique cup, league and championship treble in 1980, the cup in 1981 and the league and championship in 1982.

At 5 ft 11 ins, Saunders is three inches taller than Byrd, but, like Byrd, his ball-handling skills made him an immediate crowd-pleaser in his first season with Birmingham. Brooklyn-born Saunders was also voted the league's MVP after helping Birmingham reach the cup and championship finals.

So how do the game's two outstanding guards compare?

I've played with Alton Byrd and against him, and I've played against Russ and seen him on television, so I know their styles pretty well. They're obviously both very talented players and it's hard to pinpoint what makes either better than the other.

The basic difference is that while Russ is probably a better shooter than Alton, and looks to score more often, Alton is more of a play-maker. As a team-oriented player myself, that to me gives Alton the edge. He's always looking to run the show and make scoring chances for others.

I think his main problem has been motivation. He was at his best in his first season at Crystal Palace because he came over here not knowing what to expect and wanting to impress. But his game lost its edge when he discovered that there were no English guards, and no Americans either, who posed any threat.

He was so quick that in practice it was useless putting just one player against him because he'd just go by time after time. Putting two men on him gave him more of a challenge, and it was the same in league games. If he could get by on half his normal speed, he would.

I think the same could happen with Saunders: he's also very quick but with every season he spends here, he'll be that much less effective. He'll pick up things through experience which may improve his technique and consistency, but unless he can find a new incentive each season, I doubt he'll make the impact he did in 1982–83.

Alton has also, I believe, more body control than Russ. Whereas Russ is a better outside shooter for a little guy, Alton can go to the basket any time he chooses. I've seen him make some unbelievable moves. I'll always remember a friendly against Solent when he took a pass right under the basket with Mark Saiers right there next to him. Saiers is a foot taller and twice as wide, but Alton jumped straight up in the air, turned through 360 degrees and scored from a lay-up. I've hardly ever seen anyone else do that. I've also seen him go one-on-two in practice, like I said, and he's run the full court and then spun between these two players to lay up a nice scoop shot.

But scoring isn't the main part of Alton's game. On occasions he'll take it on himself to score more often if he thinks his team needs it.

That's what I mean when I say he's more of a play-making guard than Russ. Alton can dictate the pace, pattern and rhythm of a match. He can slow it down, speed it up, set up scoring positions for other players, or decide to score himself. But things would have to be going wrong for the team for him to take over the scoring role, and even then it can sometimes be more of a hindrance than a help. You can play one-on-five in the lower divisions, but it doesn't work too well in the First.

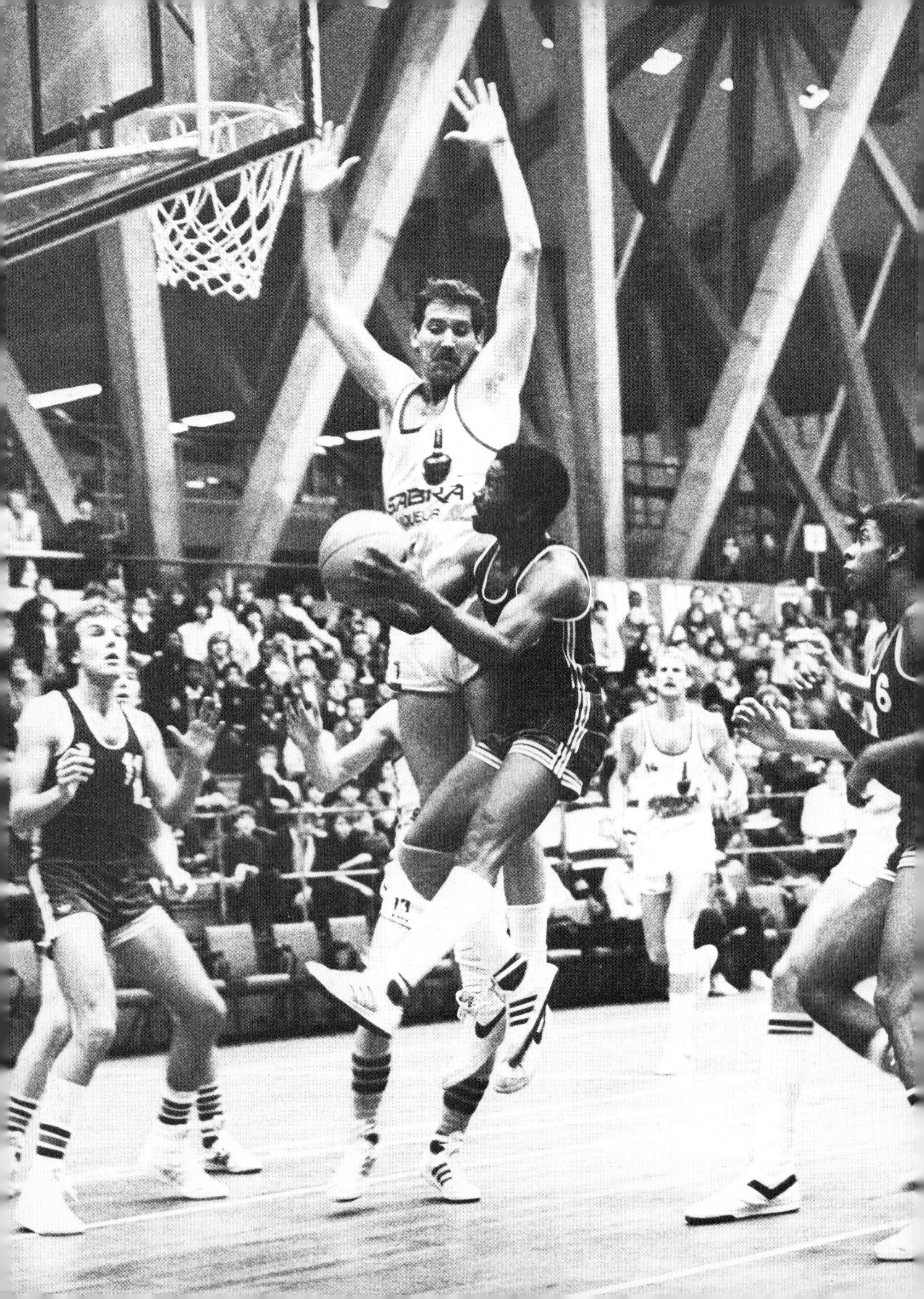

OPPOSITE: *No job's too big for Byrd*

ABOVE: *Saunders beats the Ovaltine press – head up, keeping the ball low*

Byrd, tiptoe teaser for his new team Murray against Palace

On the other hand, Russ has established himself as one of Birmingham's leading scorers and that's been a great benefit to them. But their overall team play may have suffered because they depended too heavily on him to score, instead of bringing other players into the game.

As far as passing goes, it's hard to say with Russ because Birmingham don't play the fast-break game which a guard would set up. If Russ gets the ball, he'll be looking to score himself.

With Alton it's different. Passing is one of the important aspects of his game. He has great court awareness and seems to instinctively know where his team-mates are going to be. His Palace record of 12 or 13 assists a game shows what I mean.

12 My Kind of Players

GREG McCRAY

Anyone who can come to England unknown and immediately take over Mark Saiers' title as the league's best centre must be special. At 6 ft 6 ins, my Crystal Palace team-mate Greg is a couple of inches shorter than Mark, in fact he must be one of the smallest centres around. But he makes up for that with his strength, his aggression and because he'll never back down from anyone.

McCray gets the better of Earl Williams in the Palace v Maccabi showdown

I'll always remember the Philips tournament in London after Christmas 1982 as the time Greg really earned his reputation. I was really looking forward to his match-up with Maccabi's Earl Williams. Earl the Pearl is about 6 ft 7 ins and one of the most intimidating players in Europe, certainly the most intimidating player I've ever come across. Crystal Palace met Maccabi in the final and Greg's battle with Williams was one of the spectacles of the tournament. There was a lot of talk between the two during the game. At one point Earl said: 'Hey, I'm Earl Williams, I earn 100,000 dollars a year. I'm the best in

Europe.' He tries to psyche you out. He's said the same things to me in earlier matches. But Greg wouldn't back down. He just said: 'Yeah, well you haven't played me yet.' Being his first year in Europe while Earl has been here for ages, I was impressed. And throughout the match Greg really forced Williams to play. I think Earl felt threatened himself, for a change! Greg certainly made him play one of his better games.

We lost the final, but for me it was one of the

ABOVE: *McCray keeps Williams from driving to the basket*
OPPOSITE: *McCray v Robinson in a Solent v Palace cup match*

most memorable events of the season. Apart from our win over Real Madrid, it was our best performance. I was glad to have someone like Greg around.

Another confrontation which showed Greg's

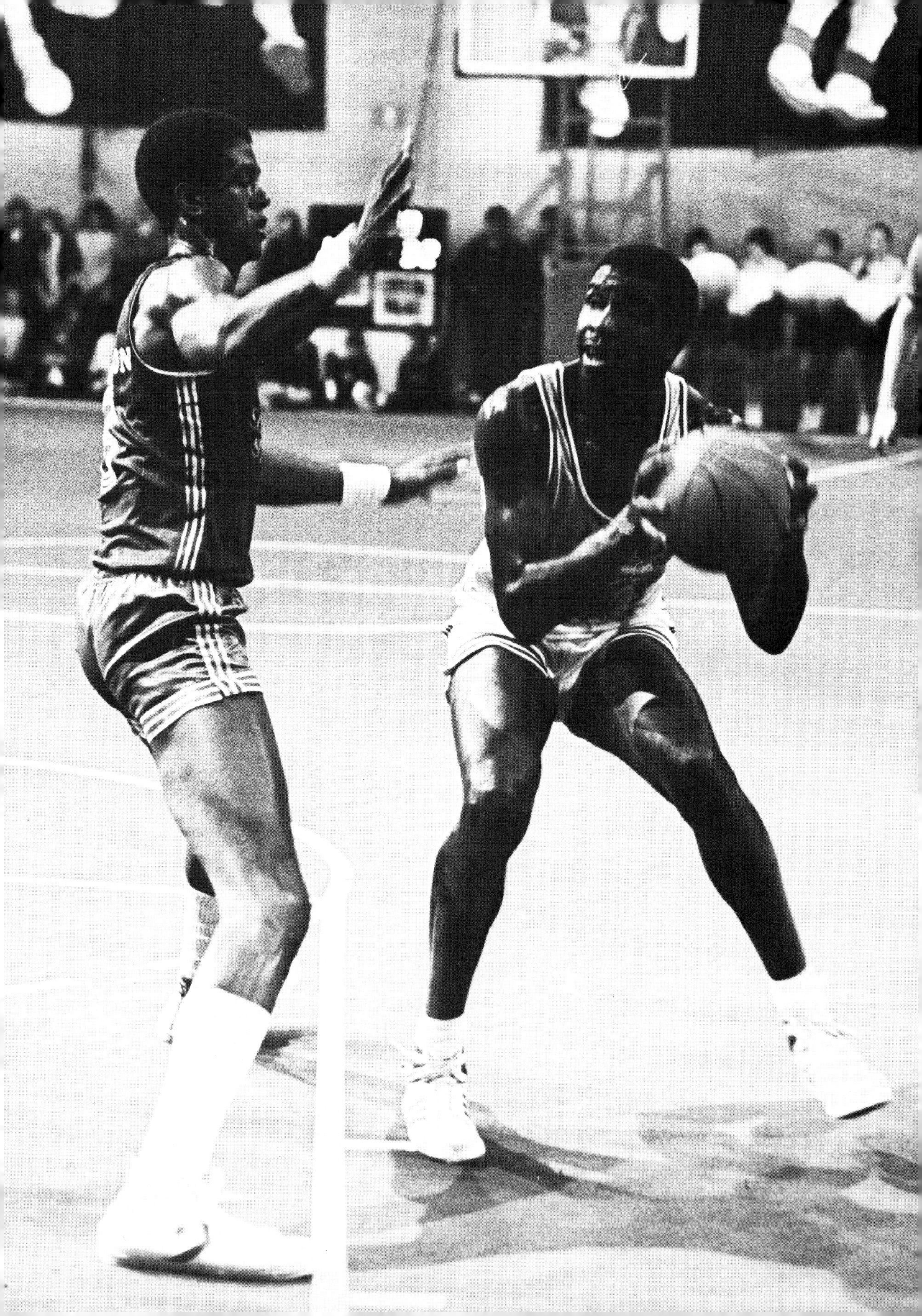

character came during our league match with Solent towards the end of the 1982–83 season.

T. J. Robinson was their centre. He's 6 ft 8 ins and a hard player. Solent had already beaten us twice during the season, in the league and the cup, so Greg was getting himself ready for this one. I remember hearing him say on the morning of the game: 'I'm gonna bust someone tonight.' He didn't say who, but it was pretty obvious that if Robinson stepped out of line and got away with it, Greg was going to take the law into his own hands.

The first half came and Robinson took a couple of shots but he wasn't hurting us. Then he missed a short jump shot, came in to follow it and Greg had him boxed out. Robinson pushed him in the back of the head and held his arm. Greg turned round and went after him. I thought, this is it, Greg's going to get himself sent off. But he didn't hit Robinson, he just grabbed him and held on.

Robinson had been trying it on for most of the season and Greg just wanted him to know that this time it was different. They both got sent off, but I felt Greg was justified in his action. Being aggressive is one thing but I've never seen Greg overstep the mark. He uses his strength to his advantage. Some players, like Alton Byrd and Russ Saunders, use their quickness, others use their height. But for Greg, strength is a big part of his game.

Having a player like that has transformed us. We're not a very tall side so we have to make up for that with more aggression, and it's that quality which Greg has given us. When you see him in there taking the rebounds, it's an inspiration to everyone else.

Greg isn't really a scoring centre in the way Bob Roma was the previous season but there have been times when he scored 27 points or so, and for a defensive centre that's not bad. But his forte is defence and rebounding and that's shown in our stats when we won the 1983 league title. We had the lowest points-against total of all the teams and even Solent managed only 73 against us in that league match. For a high-scoring team, like Solent, that says a lot for our defence. And it's having Greg McCray which makes it that way.

PAUL STIMPSON – THE BEST OF BRITISH

I'll always remember our league match against Solent towards the end of the 1982–83 season. That's not just because we avenged two defeats by them in the league and cup earlier in the season or because McCray and Robinson were sent off. It was also the night my Palace teammate Paul Stimpson showed how he's developed into the complete player.

A few years back it may have been true that English players lacked the skills, technique and attitude of Americans, but that's no longer the case. Players like Paul have made such rapid progress that they'd now get into any team here on merit alone. They're all guards because that's the position in which English players have been allowed to develop without being threatened or pushed to one side by American players.

I've watched Paul Stimpson develop over the four seasons I've been at Palace, and I like to think that he's come on so well because he's been in a very American environment! Pete Jeremich and myself both learned our basketball in the States and we've had Alton Byrd, Bob Roma, Dave Shutts, Greg McCray and several other Americans at the club, who I'm sure have all helped Paul without threatening his team place.

Paul's forte has always been his shooting. His ball handling and passing were once the weakest part of his game; he'd give the ball away and generally lacked the consistency of a good all-round player. But he's always been keen to learn, asked questions and practised hard to improve. He used to ask me a lot about defence, particularly in fast break drills where he'd want to know what he should be doing.

Another player who helped him a lot was Alton Byrd. Alton was at Palace for three years and was always either playing with Paul or against him. Although that meant Paul letting Alton run the offence while all he had to do was run down court and get ready to take a shot, it's a great learning experience just playing with someone of Alton's ability.

When Alton left, Paul took on greater responsibility for running the offence. He's become much more aggressive, both offensively and defensively, and his passing and dribbling

McCray weighs up a bounce pass

Stimpson v Saunders in a battle of the guards

are now much stronger parts of his play.

He has a great appetite for the game, which I like to see. The England team, the World Student Games, club tours, league games – any opportunity to play basketball and he's there. All that experience is now starting to show. He's confident on the ball and the fact of having an American guard alongside him doesn't affect or inhibit his play in the way that it might have done in the past. He can now play whichever role is required knowing he has the ability and experience to do it.

The game against Solent was, for me, the one where it all came together for him. We were talking about it some time later and he told me his hands were really tingling that night. He wanted the ball no matter who was covering him and he really took Solent apart. It was a crucial performance because we'd lost McCray and everyone was having to work that much

Paul Stimpson challenged by Doncaster's Ian Day

harder to fill the gap. I watched the video afterwards and time and again Paul was in there defensively, taking steals, making deflections and generally playing more aggressively than I'd ever seen him. Offensively, if they were blocking his shots he'd drive to the basket instead, draw the foul with a fake and score from the free-throw line that way!

The stats tell their own story: he was our top scorer with 22 points (67 per cent from the field, 86 per cent from the free-throw line), seven assists, five rebounds and three steals.

Although I was disappointed to lose the England captaincy, nobody was more pleased than me when it was awarded to Paul at the end of the 1983 season. He has earned it and I know he'll carry the honour with distinction. Paul is still only 24 and I've no doubt he is going to become England's own first superstar player.

13 Stars and Stripes

Basketball is the only major spectator sport that originates in the United States, and it has proved widely exportable. Today the game is played in more than 150 countries and by more than 100 million people. But while it is as popular in Leningrad as in Los Angeles, the United States continues to be the powerhouse: here the big names, big games and big money are to be found.

There are two levels that matter: the college game under the National Collegiate Athletic Association (NCAA) which attracts crowds of up to 60,000, and the million-dollar world of the professionals in the National Basketball Association (NBA) to whose ranks the college players aspire.

Competition is fierce and from the thousands

JULIUS ERVING
PHILADELPHIA 76ers

JULIUS ERVING
PHILADELPHIA 76ers

of college players who graduate every year, probably less than one hundred are chosen. Selections are made through a nationwide network of 'camps' where players go through a series of 'drafts' or 'cuts' for a particular club until the lucky few remain.

One significant development that Naismith didn't foresee in his equal-opportunity ideal was the advantage his game would give to the tall player. To be under 2 metres (6 ft 7 ins), particularly in the US game, is considered on the short side and it's the selective advantage of height that some people outside the sport consider freakish. But as any player or coach will tell you, being tall isn't enough. To get through the gruelling eighty-match season of the American professionals requires superb fitness and stamina.

In the showbiz traditions of all American sports every team and nearly every player has a nickname, with the Los Angeles Lakers, the Boston Celtics, the New York Knicks (short for Knickerbockers) and the Philadelphia 76ers among the best-known clubs.

Names like Wilt 'the Stilt' Chamberlain, Earvin 'Magic' Johnson and Julius 'Dr J' Erving may be unfamiliar in most English homes, but in the United States they're as much household names as Bobby Charlton and Lester Piggott are here.

Perhaps the player who typifies the best of both college and professional worlds is Kareem Abdul Jabbar. As plain Lew Alcindor, he helped the University College of Los Angeles (UCLA) dominate the college league during the 1960s. Then came a change of name, a change of team and an amazing change of luck for his new side, the Milwaukee Bucks. Alcindor became the bas-

KAREEM ABDUL-JABBAR

LOS ANGELES LAKERS

OSCAR ROBERTSON
GUARD   6'5"

MILWAUKEE BUCKS

OSCAR P. ROBERTSON 1938-

ketball equivalent of Muhammad Ali, became a Muslim and changed his name to Kareem Abdul Jabbar. Milwaukee had just finished bottom of the NBA but within two years, thanks to Jabbar and the ball-handling skills of Oscar 'Big O' Robertson, they won the 1971 championship. Jabbar's name continued to hit the headlines, on and off the court, following a move to Los Angeles Lakers. He was unwittingly dragged into a power struggle between black Muslim sects which ended in mass murder. But Jabbar came through a traumatic period in his career to become one of America's all-time greats. He is the NBA's second-highest aggregate scorer with more than 28,000 points, only 3,000 behind Wilt Chamberlain, and has been in four NBA championship-winning sides.

Now there is a new name emerging to challenge Jabbar. He's Ralph Sampson, another college prodigy who at 7 ft 4 ins is two inches taller. Sampson won three successive 'College Player of the Year' awards with Virginia University before joining the pro ranks in the autumn of 1983 as the most sought-after student in years.

On the subject of feats, the now-retired Chamberlain holds 21 NBA records, scored 50 points on no less than 122 occasions, and in 1962 scored 100 for the Philadelphia Warriors.

In the United States you're not a champion until you've won a series of play-offs between the top finishers in the league. The play-offs are the highlight of the season in the college and professional game.

The Boston Celtics are far and away the most successful NBA team with 14 titles, eight of them in successive years between 1959 and 1966. Among the colleges, UCLA are top dogs with ten wins. With some 80 league games behind them plus another 20 or so in the play-offs, it's no wonder that the NBA winners are proclaimed

MAGIC JOHNSON

world champions. The fact is that as the only one hundred per cent professional league in the world, the NBA has no challengers. There is an official world championship but it's a non-pro event and the American representatives comprise the best of the college players.

The highest-paid player in American basketball is 'Magic' Johnson, who at the age of 21 signed a 25-year contract worth 25 million dollars (about £14 million) with the Los Angeles Lakers. Such is Johnson's clout that when he criticised the club coach for boring tactics during a 1982 run of five straight wins, the coach was fired the next morning. Car stickers quickly appeared all over Los Angeles: 'How do you make a coach disappear? Magic!'

When it comes to flying the flag abroad, you'll be lucky to see any of these superstars or their teams outside their homeland. That job is left to the show business wing of the NBA known as the Harlem Globetrotters. Now that is a name familiar in households in Britain and the world over because of the breathtaking skills and pure entertainment they have brought to millions. The Globetrotters were founded in Chicago by London-born Abe Saperstein in 1927. After winning every title in the book, they set out on a world crusade which has taken them to nearly 100 countries. They've been watched by more than 80 million people and in 1951 attracted basketball's biggest-ever crowd – 75,000 in Berlin's Olympic stadium. Buckets of water, boxing gloves and joke balls are all part of the act, but so too are the skills of players like 'Curly' Neal, whose dribbling displays are one of the main attractions, and 'Meadowlark' Lemon, who is famous for his long-distance overarm shots.

The face of basketball has been changing down the years. It started white but now it's almost entirely black, particularly in the NBA.

MILESTONES 1891–1980

1891 Dr James Naismith invented the game of basket ball.
1892 First public game played between students and teachers at the School for Christian Workers, Springfield, Mass. The students won 5–1 in front of a crowd of 200.
1893 Backboards introduced to prevent interference by spectators. Metal rims replaced peach baskets. First women's match, at Northampton, Mass. No men were allowed to watch the game!
1894 Soccer balls replaced by basket balls. Free throws introduced.
1895 Field goal changed from three to two points; foul shots from three to one point.
1897 Five-man teams became general practice.
1898 First professional league formed in United States called the National Basketball League.
1904 Outdoor exhibition by college teams at the St Louis Olympics.
1905 Columbia claimed first national title by beating Minnesota and Wisconsin.
1910 Glass backboards first approved.
1921 Basket ball became one word.
1923 Person fouled had to shoot the foul shot; eliminated the 'designated foul-shooter'.
1927 Harlem Globetrotters formed by London-born Abe Saperstein.
1929 The 'cage' (rope or chicken wire round the court) was abolished.
1930 Double referee system introduced.
1931 Tournament in Peking attracted 70,000 fans over three nights.
1932 International federation (FIBA) founded in Geneva.

Miss Senda Berenson, in long dress, with Smith College students in Northampton, Massachusetts, where women played their first public basketball game on 22 March 1893

1936 First Olympic title won by United States.
1937 Centre jump after each score eliminated.
1939 Death of Dr James Naismith. University of Oregon won first NCAA title.
1944 Time-outs increased from four to five; unlimited substitutions; five-personal-foul limit.
1946 Jump shot first used by Wyoming University player Kenny Sailors. College basketball's first 20,000 crowd at Chicago.
1949 National Basketball League merged with Basketball Association of America to form the National Basketball Association (NBA).
1950 Charles Cooper of Duquesne became first black player in NBA, drafted by Boston Celtics.
1951 An all-time record 75,000 saw Harlem Globetrotters in Berlin's Olympic stadium.
1956 A record seven overtimes played by college teams Black Hills and Yankton.
1962 Wilt Chamberlain scored 100 points for Philadelphia against New York.
1967 Professional distance record for a field goal set by Jerry Harkness of Indiana with 92-ft shot.
1969 Lew Alcindor, later to become Kareem Abdul Jabbar, became first player to win three successive NCAA MVP awards for UCLA. Boston Celtics won 11th NBA championship in 13 years.
1972 United States lost Olympic title for first time, beaten by Russia in Munich.
1974 North Carolina State won NCAA title to end UCLA's record of seven straight wins. Moses Malone became the first player to move directly from high school to pro ranks by joining Utah Stars.
1975 Pro basketball's highest-scoring game – San Diego 176, New York Nets 166.
1976 Women's basketball became Olympic event. Soviet Union won the gold.
1980 NBA adopted three points for a field goal. Ann Meyers first woman to sign for NBA but didn't make Indiana Pacers team. Pro basketball's biggest crowd of 40,172 saw Milwaukee beat Seattle 108-97.

Wilt Chamberlain

14 Around the World

Basketball's first Olympic final flew in the face of Naismith's concept of the game as an indoor sport and suffered as a result. An outdoor surface of sand and earth turned soggy in a rainstorm and reduced the match between the United States and Canada to a mudbath. The 19-8 scoreline to the Americans reflected the level of the play possible.

That was in Berlin in 1936, just four years after the formation of the game's international governing body, FIBA (Fédération Internationale de Basketball Amateur). Basketball had been demonstrated at the Olympics as early as 1904, at the St Louis Games, and FIBA was founded to promote international competition. The 1936 Olympics were its first major success and Naismith, by now a world ambassador for the sport, was there to present the medals.

With two exceptions, the United States have not surprisingly dominated the world game. They didn't compete in the 1980 Moscow Games in protest at the Soviet Union's involvement in Afghanistan and in 1972 at Munich they lost to the Soviet Union in the most astonishing finish in the history of the sport.

With a minute to go, the Americans had reduced a ten-point deficit to just two when Russia's Alexander Belov was fouled in the act of shooting. With the score 48-46, Belov scored one of his three free throws to increase Russia's lead to 49-46. With the game 40 playing seconds from finishing, the Americans reduced the deficit to 49-48 and with only ten seconds left, they forced a turnover. From the resulting possession they drew a foul that gave them two vital free throws. They had already levelled the scores at 49-49 when the Russians called a time-out. But the Americans ignored it, completed their second free throw and took the lead for the first time at 50-49, with the Russians protesting.

Play restarted with three seconds remaining, but amid the confusion the referee wasn't satisfied and ordered a fresh start from the endline. However, the clock, which showed only one second left, wasn't reset and time elapsed with the Americans celebrating what they thought was a famous victory. But the match commissioner, Dr William Jones, wasn't satisfied and ordered another restart, this time with the clock showing the correct time. The Russians lobbed a high ball down court, Alexander Belov took the crucial catch under the American basket to set the final three seconds ticking away, and almost in the same motion sunk the winning basket on the final buzzer. The Russians won 51-50 and, despite their protests, the Americans lost an Olympic final for the first and only time.

While the United States Olympic team comprises largely college players, internationals throughout the rest of the world, except in the Iron Curtain countries, are able to play in professional leagues while maintaining their Olympic status. The safeguard is that they are paid not only for playing but for activities such as coaching and administration. As long as basketball does not provide their only or main source of income, Olympic status is maintained.

In addition to the Olympics*, there is also a world championship held every four years. Argentina were hosts for the first event in 1950 when they won their one and only title. Russia, Yugoslavia and Brazil have each won the tournament twice, while the United States have won

* For the Olympic Games Great Britain enters a combined team from the four home nations, although this has not yet succeeded in getting beyond the qualifying stages except in 1948 when Britain were hosts.

OPPOSITE: *Aulcie Perry (8) of Maccabi wins a rebounding duel with Groningen's Al Faber*

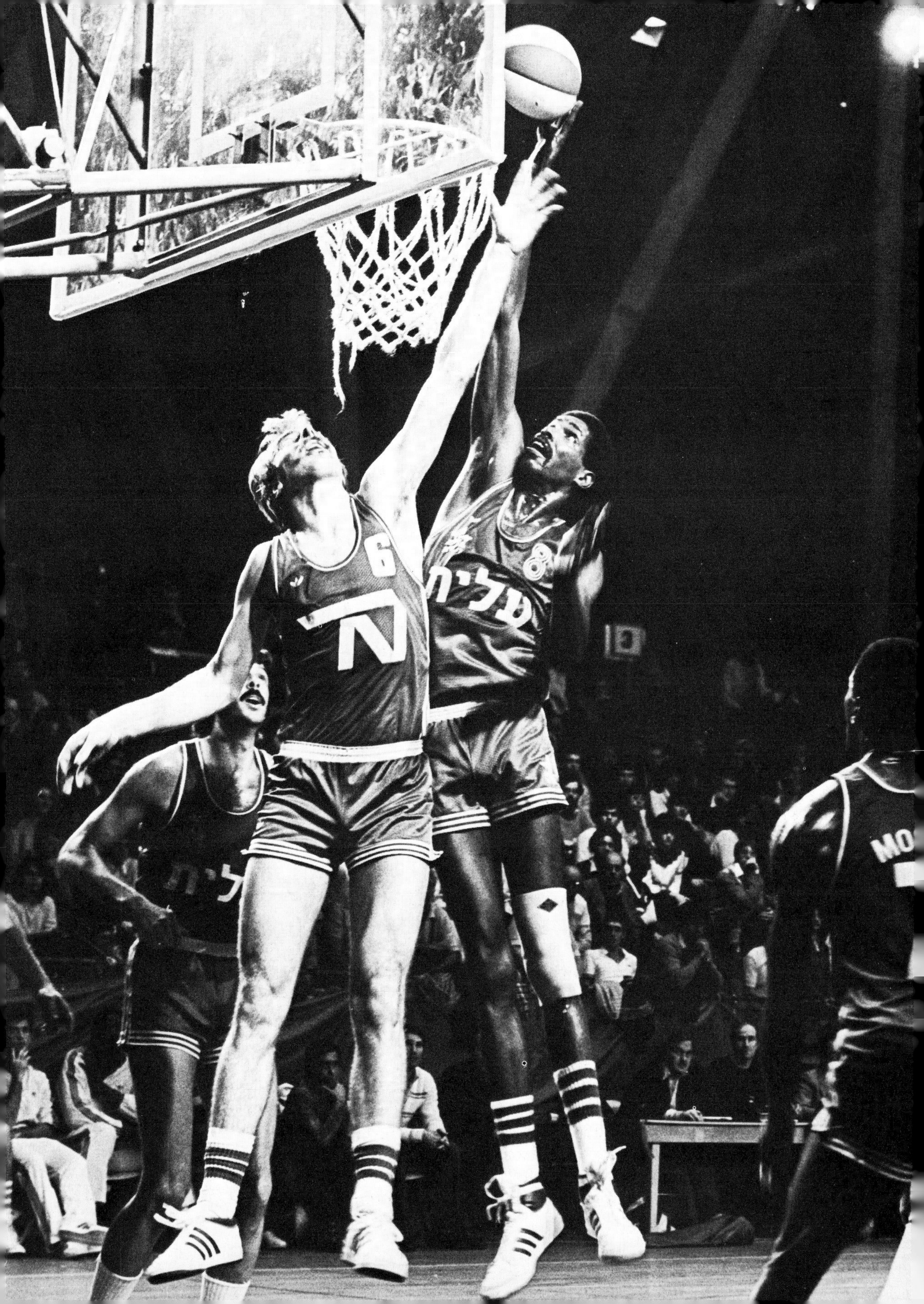
עלית

it once. At the 1978 championships they were represented by the college side Athletes in Action, a team of basketball-playing crusaders who preach the gospel to fans during intervals. They managed only fifth place but showed their power as a club side when they won the 1980 Philips international tournament at Crystal Palace. Their former leading player, 7 ft 1 in. Ralph Drollinger, declined an offer of £250,000 for a three-year spell with the New Jersey Nets because it was incompatible with his faith.

Tragedy struck the Soviet camp before the 1978 championship with the death of their Munich hero Alexander Belov, and they were beaten in the final by Yugoslavia.

In Europe only Italy and Israel have seriously challenged the domination of the Soviet Union and Yugoslavia, the latter with the help of naturalised Americans. Indeed, wherever you look in basketball countries outside the Iron Curtain, it's hard to escape the ubiquitous American presence. Such is the omnipotence of their basketball that other countries will seek any connection to get American-raised players into their own national sides.

There are three principal competitions in European club basketball: the European Cup, which is competed for by the champion side of each country (the champions being either the winners of an American-style end-of-season play-off between the top finishers in the league or, as in England from 1984, the league title winners themselves); the Cup-winners' Cup, for the winners of national cup competitions; and the Korac Cup, the equivalent of soccer's UEFA Cup, for the other leading league sides.

Naturalised Americans Wayne Brabender and Clifford Luyk were the driving force behind Spanish club Real Madrid in their sweep towards a record seven wins in the European Cup during the 1970s. Probably the most famous American export was Bill Bradley, a former college star and Olympic gold medallist who commuted between Oxford University, where he was on a scholarship, and Milan, whom he helped win the European Cup in 1966. On his return to the United States, Bradley turned professional and helped the New York Knicks to the NBA title.

Outside the NBA, the Italian league is the richest, with several players on contracts worth up to £60,000 a season. In England the salary range is between £5,000 and £25,000, with only a handful of top Americans commanding the higher figure.

With the influx of Americans, FIBA has had to impose limits on their number at club and international level with players sometimes having to serve lengthy residential periods before qualifying. European clubs are generally restricted to two Americans, although they are often effectively able to double that number by also being allowed to field players with dual national status.

However, basketball isn't without a great many outstanding home-grown players to match the thrills and skills of the Ervings and Jabbars of the NBA. Among them is Italian giant Dino Meneghin, who could have played in the NBA any time he wished but instead chose to help Varese reach ten successive European Cup finals between 1970 and 1979. Russia's 7 ft 4½ ins Vladimir Tkachenko and Yugoslavia's Kresimir Cosic, who learned his basketball in the United States, have been the cream of the Iron Curtain country players.

Yugoslavia's players have made such great strides recently that two of the players who helped them win the 1978 world championship, Dragen Dalipagic and Merza Delibasic, have been the foreign element of Real Madrid's recent European Cup bids.

From Asia, 7 ft 4½ ins Mu Tieh-chu showed how a little race can grow a long way when China won the Asian Games four times in a row. Mu is over 30 now, but there is a new generation of Chinese being groomed to challenge the world and six of their 12-man squad are more than 6 ft 6 ins! The Japanese are also thought to be short: their leading player is Okayama and he is 7 ft 9 ins!

OPPOSITE: *Real Madrid's Juan Corbalan*

OVERLEAF: *Werner Karabek of the Austrian side Klosterneuberg moves into action as former Crystal Palace star Bob Roma drives for the basket*

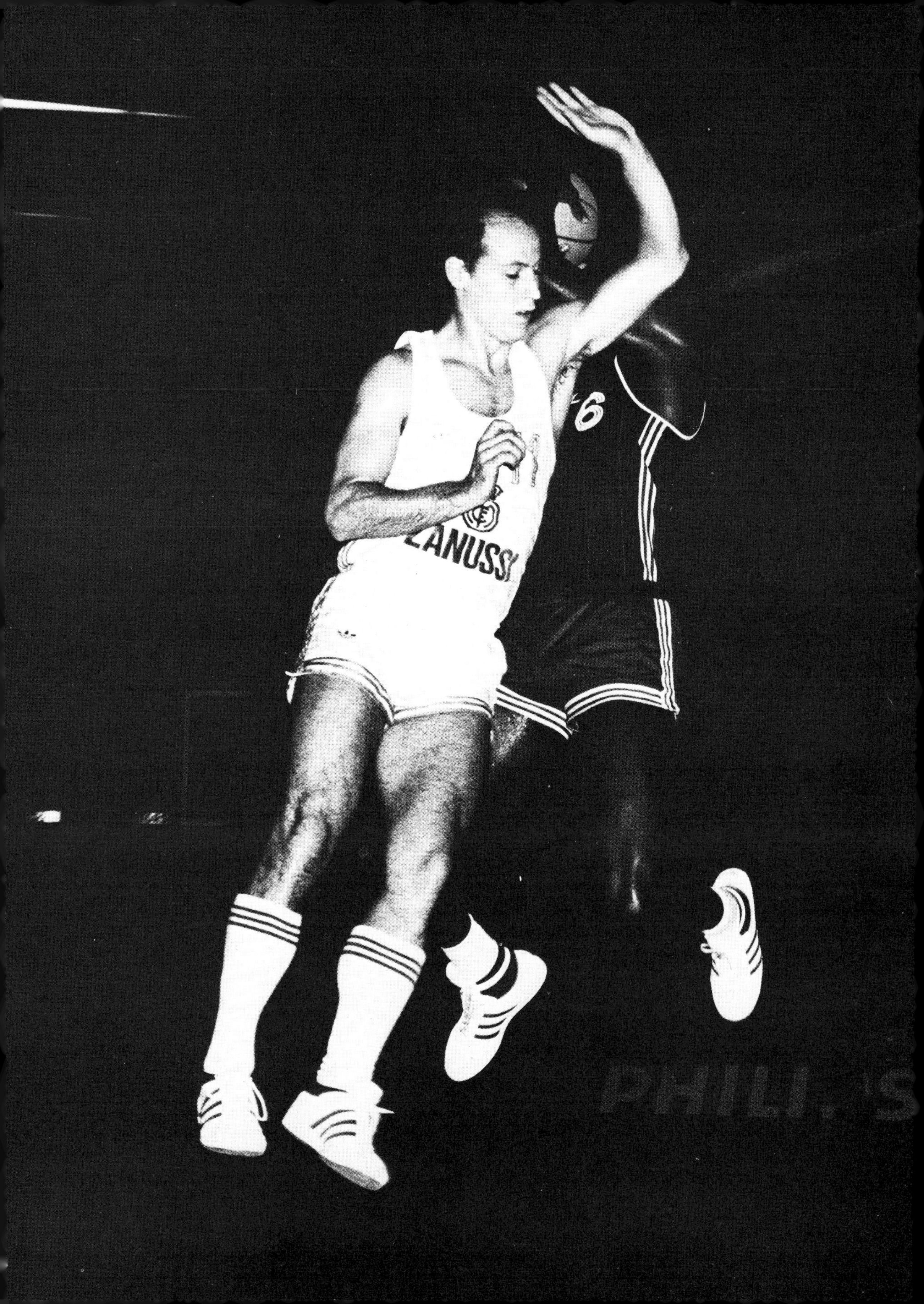

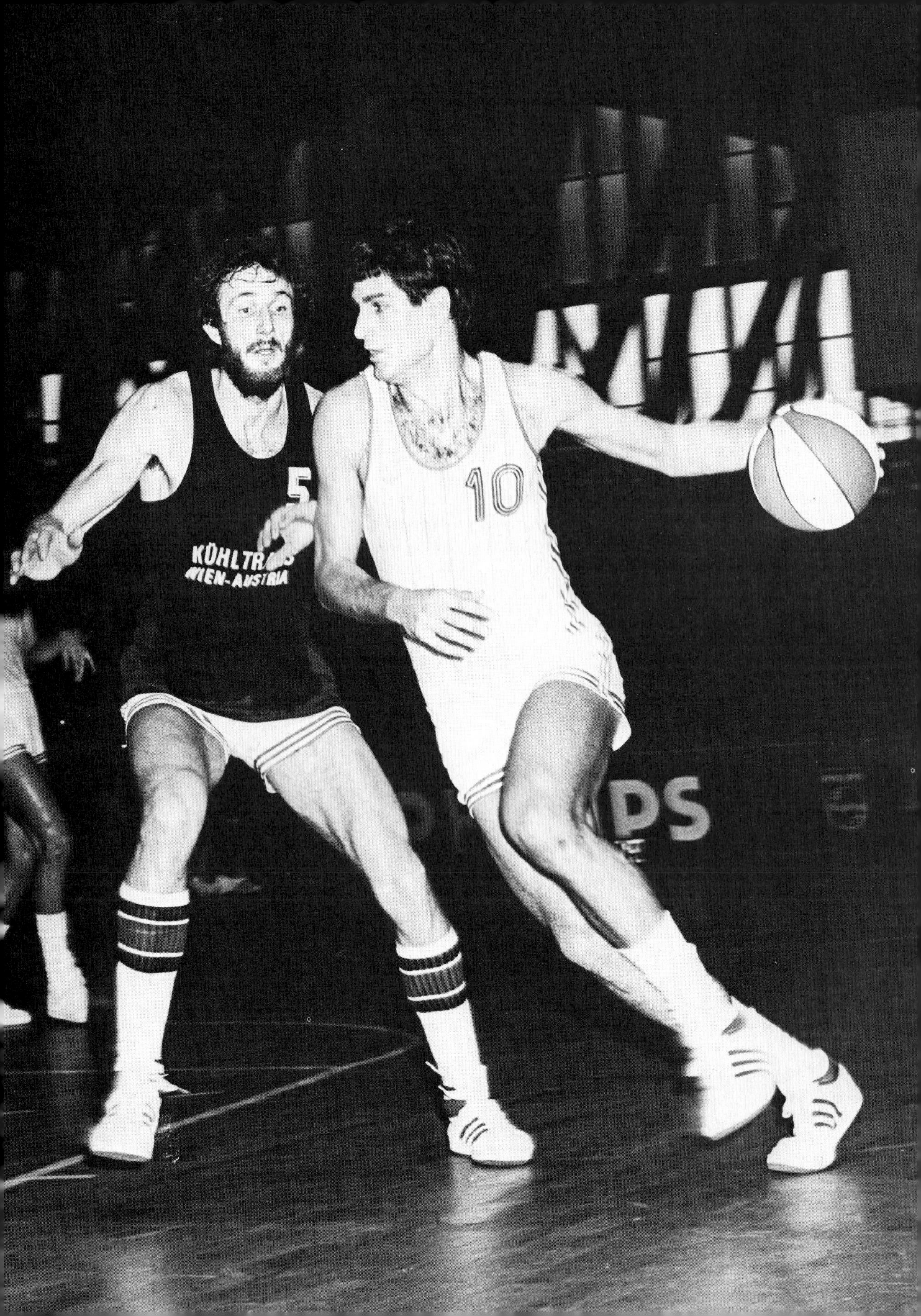
5
10

15 A-Z of Terms

Air Ball A shot that's so off-target, it doesn't even hit the rim of the basket. Also called a 'brick'.

Assist A pass leading directly to a score. Also called a 'feed'.

Backboard A flat, often transparent board to which the basket is attached at each end of the court.

Back Court The end of the court a team is trying to defend.

Back Court Violation When the attacking team pass the ball back into their own half, thus forfeiting possession.

Bank Shot An attempt to score by bouncing the ball off the backboard.

Baseball Pass A one-handed overhead pass, as used in baseball, often at the start of a fast break.

Baseline Also known as the end-line, it's the line behind the basket which is the end limit of the court.

Baseline Drive Powerful attacking drive towards the other team's basket along the end-line.

Basket The metal ring and net at each end of the court. Also denotes a field goal.

Basket Hanging The practice of staying near the opponents' basket when play is at the other end. Can produce a quick score but depletes the defence.

Blocking Illegal obstruction involving personal contact. Often incurred near the basket to prevent opposing player collecting rebound.

Boards The backboards. Also used to describe rebounds, which many coaches believe are the most critical factor of the game. Hence 'the game will be won on the boards'.

Box Out Defensive play in which defenders get between opponents and the basket to prevent an offensive rebound.

Breakaway When one or more players break away for an easy basket.

Bucket Another term for a basket.

Cager Old term for a player, from the days when basketball was played inside net cages. See 'Story of the Game'.

Charging A contact foul committed by an attacking or offensive player, usually as he drives for the basket.

Charity Stripe Another term for the free-throw line.

Court The playing area – see chapter on rules, p. 40.

D Abbreviation for defence.

Dead Ball A ball that's out of play or being used to take free throws.

Defence Pronounced dee-fence, it refers to team tactics when not in possession of the ball.

Double Foul When rival players commit fouls against each other. Result, a jump ball.

Double Team When two defenders move in on an opponent with the ball. Also called a 'trap'.

Dunk Scoring shot when a player jumps above the basket and crams the ball through the ring. Also called a 'stuff' or a 'jam'. A crowd-pleaser.

Fake A false move designed to throw an opponent off balance.

Fast Break Quick counterattack out of defence aimed at scoring before opponents have time to regroup.

Field Goal Any scoring shot other than free throws.

Filling the Lanes Players travelling up the sides and centre of the court during a fast break.

Floor Play Combined offensive and defensive performance of a team or player.

Free Throw Penalty shots worth one point each.

Front Court The half of the court which a team is attacking.

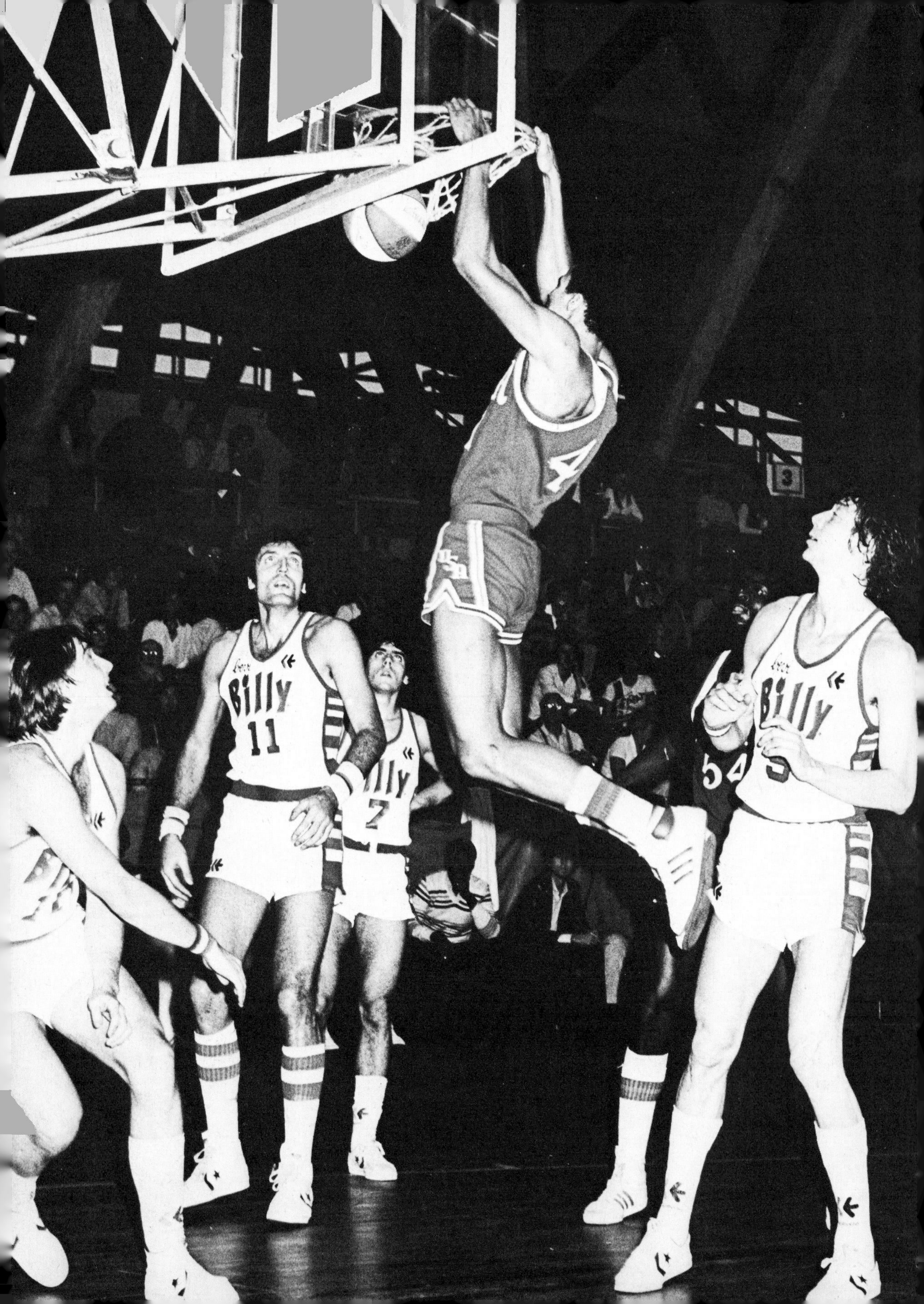
Billy
11
Billy
7
4
Billy

OPPOSITE: *The dunk, as shown by Wilbert Singleton of Athletes in Action during the Philips Tournament at Crystal Palace*

Full Court Press A pressure defence in which a team tries to regain possession by hustling the opposition over the entire court area.

Give and Go An attacking move in which a player passes and goes for the return pass or draws an opponent out of position to open up a scoring chance.

Gunning the Ball Trying to shoot too much when team-mates are better positioned.

Hook Shot A one-handed shot attempted with a wide, swinging motion when under pressure and not fully facing the basket.

Jump Ball A ball thrown up between two opposing players, either to start play at the beginning of each half or after a double foul.

Jump Shot A two-handed distance shot, attempted under pressure by trying to jump and shoot over an opponent.

Key Key-shaped area under the basket equivalent to soccer's penalty area. Attacking players are not allowed inside for more than three seconds.

Lay-up One-handed bank shot from under the basket. The simplest and easiest scoring shot.

Man-to-Man A defensive tactic in which players mark specific opponents regardless of position.

Offence Pronounced off-ence, basketball's word for attack.

One-on-One Where the attacking player faces one defensive player.

Outlet Pass to either sideline from a defensive rebound designed to get a fast break going.

Overtime Extra periods of five minutes used to produce a result if scores are level at the end of normal time.

Pick *See* post.

Post A legal non-contact obstruction in which an attacking player blocks an opponent's path in order to defend a team-mate in possession. Also called a 'pick' or a 'screen'. (From the days when basketball was played in courts with supporting pillars on the field of play.)

Press Short for pressure defence. Hence full-court press, half-court press.

Rebound Ball that bounces off backboard and is collected by a defender or attacker. Hence defensive rebound, offensive rebound.

Screen *See* post.

Slam Dunk Extra-powerful version of a dunk, risking GBH to anyone who gets in the way.

Steal Winning the ball from an opponent.

Team Fouls Individual fouls, technical or otherwise, which count as a whole against a team. Any team committing eight fouls in either half concedes two free throws for every subsequent offence against the team with the ball.

Technical Foul Term for non-contact fouls such as unsportsmanlike conduct, illegal substitution, excessive time-outs etc. Results in a free throw for the other team.

Thirty-Second Rule Team in possession must make an attempt to score within that time period or forfeit possession.

Three-for-Two Free shots awarded for fouls on players in the act of shooting. Three attempts to score two baskets, successful shots counting one point each.

Time-Out A 60-second interval which can be called twice in each half by both coaches. Usually called to change tactics or upset opponents' rhythm.

Tip-Off Start of a game.

Travelling Running with the ball, illegal dribble, resulting in loss of possession.

Turnover Losing possession without having taken a shot, usually through an interception or steal.

Violation Term for offences other than fouls, eg travelling.

Zone Defence in which players mark an area of the court rather than a specific opponent. *See also* man-to-man.

APPENDICES

1 Records

ENGLAND

MEN'S CHAMPIONSHIP FINALS

Date	Venue	Winners	Runners-up	Result
1936	Birmingham	*Hoylake YMCA*	London Poly	32–31
1937	Liverpool	*Hoylake YMCA*	Latter Day Saints	23–17
1938	Wembley	*Catford Saints*	Rochdale Greys	61–47
1939	London	*Catford Saints*	Rochdale Greys	53–41
1940	London	*Birmingham A.I.*	Central YMCA	35–30
1947	Birmingham	*Carpathians*	Birmingham D'bran	48–25
1948*	—	*Latter Day Sts*	—	–
1949*	—	*Latter Day Sts*	—	–
1950*	Nottingham	*Latter Day Sts*	USAF Burtonwood	–
1951	Nottingham	*Birmingham D'bran*	London Poly	34–33
1952	Wembley	*London Poly*	Birmingham D'bran	40–29
1953	Manchester	*London Poly*	Birmingham D'bran	55–46
1954	Birmingham	*London Poly*	Nottingham YMCA	98–53
1955	London	*London Poly*	Birmingham D'bran	58–54
1956*	Brighton	*USAF Lakenheath*	US Navy	–
1957	London	*Central YMCA*	London Poly	63–51
1958	London	*Central YMCA*	East Ham	48–40
1959	Leicester	*Aspley Old Boys*	Birmingham D'bran	58–39
1960	Birmingham	*Central YMCA*	London Poly	95–62
1961	South Ruislip	*London Univ.*	Central YMCA	68–59
1962	South Ruislip	*Central YMCA*	RAE Eagles	87–47
1963	Albert Hall	*Central YMCA*	London Univ.	70–69
1964	Albert Hall	*Central YMCA*	London Univ.	78–56
1965	Crystal Palace	*Aldershot*	Oxford Univ.	79–63
1966	Crystal Palace	*Oxford Univ.*	Aldershot	91–70
1967	Crystal Palace	*Central YMCA*	Vauxhall Motors	64–62
1968	Crystal Palace	*Oxford Univ.*	Aldershot	61–59
1969	Crystal Palace	*Central YMCA*	Aldershot	70–62
1970	Crystal Palace	*Liverpool Police*	Oxford Univ.	73–67
1971	Crystal Palace	*Manchester Univ.*	Sutton	88–81
1972	Crystal Palace	*Avenue*	Cambridge	78–66
1973	Crystal Palace	*London Latvians SK*	Sutton	70–69
1974	Crystal Palace	*Sutton and CP*	Embassy	120–100
1975	Wembley	*Embassy*	Sutton and CP	82–81
1976	Wembley	*Cinzano SCP*	Embassy	108–88
1977	Wembley	*Cinzano SCP*	Embassy	91–90

* records incomplete

Date	Venue	Winners	Runners-up	Result
1978	Wembley	*Cinzano SCP*	Team Fiat	89–87
1979	Wembley	*Crystal Palace*	Team Fiat	75–63
1980	Wembley	*Crystal Palace*	Team Fiat	93–83
1981	Wembley	*Sunderland*	Crystal Palace	96–92
1982	Wembley	*Crystal Palace*	Sunderland	111–86
1983	Wembley	*Sunderland*	Crystal Palace	75–74

NATIONAL LEAGUE DIVISION ONE – MEN

Season	Winners	Season	Winners
1973	Avenue (Leyton)	1979	Doncaster
1974	C. Palace	1980	C. Palace
1975	E.A.S. Islington	1981	T.F. Birmingham
1976	C. Palace	1982	C. Palace
1977	C. Palace	1983	C. Palace
1978	C. Palace		

NATIONAL LEAGUE DIVISION TWO – MEN

Season	Winners	Season	Winners
1976	V.M. Bedford	1980	Nottingham
1977	Stockport B.	1981	Solent
1978	Epab Sunderland	1982	Leicester
1979	S.P. Guildford	1983	Bolton

COACH OF THE YEAR

1977	K. Tober	1981	T. Becker
1978	W. Beswick	1982	T. Wisman
1979	M. Wordsworth	1983	D. Palmer
1980	V. Tinsley		

NBL MOST VALUABLE PLAYER

1977	Allen Bunting (Metros)	1981	Alton Byrd (C. Palace)
1978	Rick Mack (Metros)	1982	Mark Saiers (Solent)
1979	Bobby Cooper (Metros)	1983	Russ Saunders (Birmingham)
1980	Alton Byrd (C. Palace)		

MEN'S CUP FINALS

Date	Venue	Winners	Runners-up	Result
1979	Sheffield	*Doncaster*	Crystal Palace	73–71
1980	Sheffield	*Crystal Palace*	Doncaster	97–67
1981	Coventry	*Crystal Palace*	Doncaster	91–74
1982	Leicester	*Solent*	Doncaster	127–91
1983	Leicester	*Solent*	Birmingham	98–97

FIRST DIVISION RECORD-BREAKERS

Most points in a game (team): **165** by Crystal Palace v Vauxhall 3-12-77.
Most points in a game (individual): **68** by Bobby Cooper (London YMCA) v Exeter 2-3-79.
Most points in a season: **732** (average 36.6) by Bobby Cooper (London YMCA) 1978/79.

WOMEN'S CHAMPIONSHIP FINALS

Date	Venue	Winners	Runners-up	Result
1981	Wembley	Southgate	Crystal Palace	59-48
1982	Wembley	Southgate	Northampton	67-61
1983	Wembley	Southgate	Northampton	53-51

WOMEN'S CUP FINAL

Date	Venue	Winners	Runners-up	Result
1965	RAF Stanmore	Malory	Sheffield Hatters	42-24
1966	Stoke-on-Trent	Malory	London Unicorns	48-45
1967	RAF Stanmore	Malory	London Unicorns	50-48
1968	Bracknell	Abbey Wood*	Malory	2-0
1969	Bracknell	Malory	St. Mary's, Cheltenham	59-41
1970	Bracknell	Abbey Wood	Eston Tigers	65-53
1971	Leeds	Abbey Wood	Turnford Tigers	45-41
1972	Leeds	Turnford Tigers	Abbey Wood	59-50
1973	Bracknell	Turnford Tigers	Eston Eagles	73-64
1974	Walsall	Eston Eagles	Turnford Tigers	56-37
1975	Edmonton	Cleveland Eagles	Turnford Tigers	48-44
1976	Edmonton	Turnford Tigers	Cleveland Eagles	47-40
1977	Wembley	Tigers	Cleveland Eagles	64-62
1978	Wembley	Tigers	Cleveland Eagles	60-59
1979	Hinckley	Tigers	Corvus Luton	65-50
1980	Wembley	Tigers	Corvus Luton	91-48
1981	(two legs)	Southgate	Crystal Palace	145-137
1982	(two legs)	Tigers	Northampton	91-89
1983	(two legs)	Southgate	Northampton	144-142

* Won by default after opponents fielded an ineligible player

NATIONAL LEAGUE DIVISION ONE – WOMEN

Season	Winners	Season	Winners
1976	Turnford Tigers	1980	Tigers
1977	Tigers	1981	Southgate
1978	Cleveland Eagles	1982	Southgate
1979	Eagles	1983	Southgate

WOMEN'S RECORD-BREAKERS

Most points in a game (team): **152** by Tigers v Waltham Abbey 17-2-79.
Most points in a game (individual): **58** by Anne Gollogly (Cleveland Eagles) v Waltham Abbey 4-2-79.

WOMEN'S PLAYER OF THE YEAR

1975	Jacki Wainwright (Tigers)	1979	Pauline Birch (Tigers)
1976	Anne Gollogly (Eagles)	1980	Joy Ackland (Tigers)
1977	Andrea Warner (Tigers)	1981	Joy Ackland (Tigers)
1978	Joan Last (Tigers)	1982	No award

MAJOR EUROPEAN RESULTS

EUROPEAN CHAMPIONSHIP WINNERS

Date	Venue	Men	Women
1935	Geneva	Latvia	–
1937	Riga	Lithuania	–
1938	Rome	–	Italy
1939	Kaunus	Lithuania	–
1946	Geneva	Czechoslovakia	–
1947	Prague	Soviet Union	–
1949	Cairo	Egypt	–
1950	Budapest	–	Soviet Union
1951	Paris	Soviet Union	–
1952	Moscow	–	Soviet Union
1953	Moscow	Soviet Union	–
1954	Belgrade	–	Soviet Union
1955	Budapest	Hungary	–
1956	Prague	–	Soviet Union
1957	Sofia	Soviet Union	–
1958	Lodz	–	Bulgaria
1959	Istanbul	Soviet Union	–
1960	Sofia	–	Soviet Union
1961	Belgrade	Soviet Union	–
1962	Mulhouse	–	Soviet Union
1963	Wroclaw	Soviet Union	–
1964	Budapest	–	Soviet Union
1965	Moscow	Soviet Union	–
1966	Sibiu-Cluj	–	Soviet Union
1967	Helsinki	Soviet Union	–
1968	Messina	–	Soviet Union
1969	Naples	Soviet Union	–
1970	Rotterdam	–	Soviet Union
1971	Essen	Soviet Union	–
1972	Varna	–	Soviet Union
1973	Barcelona	Yugoslavia	–
1974	Cagliari	–	Soviet Union
1975	Belgrade	Yugoslavia	–
1976	Clermont-Ferrand	–	Soviet Union
1977	Liege	Yugoslavia	–
1978	Poznan	–	Soviet Union
1979	Turin	Soviet Union	–
1980	Banja Luka	—	Soviet Union
1981	Prague	Soviet Union	–
1981	Ancona	—	Soviet Union
1983	Nantes	Italy	—

MEN'S CLUB CHAMPIONSHIP WINNERS

Date	European Cup	Cup-winners' Cup	Korac Cup
1958	ASK Riga (Sov)	–	–
1959	ASK Riga	–	–
1960	ASK Riga	–	–
1961	TSKA Moscow	–	–
1962	Dynamo Tbilisi	–	–
1963	TSKA Moscow	–	–
1964	Real Madrid	–	–
1965	Real Madrid	–	–
1966	Milan	–	–
1967	Real Madrid	Varese (Italy)	–
1968	Real Madrid	AEK Athens	–
1969	TSKA Moscow	Slavia Prague	–
1970	Varese	Fides Naples	–
1971	TSKA Moscow	Milan	–
1972	Varese	Milan	–
1973	Varese	Spartak Leningrad	Forst Cantu (Italy)
1974	Real Madrid	Red Star Belgrade	Forst Cantu
1975	Varese	Spartak Leningrad	Forst Cantu
1976	Varese	Milan	Jugoplastika (Yug)
1977	Maccabi Tel Aviv	Cantu	Jugoplastika
1978	Real Madrid	Cantu	Partizan Belgrade
1979	Bosna Sarajevo (Yug)	Cantu	Partizan
1980	Real Madrid	Varese	Arrigoni Rieti (Italy)
1981	Maccabi Tel Aviv	Cantu	Juventud Badalona
1982	Cantu	Cibona Zagreb	Limoges
1983	Cantu	Scavolini Pesaro	Limoges

WOMEN'S CHAMPIONSHIP WINNERS

Date	European Cup	Ronchetti Cup
1959	Slavia Sofia	–
1960	Daugawa Riga (Sov)	–
1961	Daugawa Riga	–
1962	Daugawa Riga	–
1963	Slavia Sofia	–
1964	Daugawa Riga	–
1965	Daugawa Riga	–
1966	Daugawa Riga	–
1967	Daugawa Riga	–
1968	Daugawa Riga	–
1969	Daugawa Riga	–
1970	Daugawa Riga	–
1971	Daugawa Riga	–
1972	Daugawa Riga	–
1973	Daugawa Riga	–
1974	Daugawa Riga	–
1975	Daugawa Riga	Spartak Leningrad

Date	European Cup	Ronchetti Cup
1976	Sparta Prague	Slavia Prague
1977	Daugawa Riga	Moscow Spartak
1978	Sesto Giovanni (Ital)	Levski Spartak (Bul)
1979	Red Star Belgrade	Levski Spartak
1980	Crvena Zveda (Bul)	Monting Zagreb
1981	Daugawa Riga	Spartak Moscow
1982	Daugawa Riga	Spartak Moscow
1983	Zolu Vicenza (Ital)	BSE Budapest

NBA CHAMPIONS

1947	Philadelphia Warriors
1948	Baltimore Bullets
1949	Minneapolis Lakers
1950	Minneapolis Lakers
1951	Rochester Royals
1952	Minneapolis Lakers
1953	Minneapolis Lakers
1954	Minneapolis Lakers
1955	Syracuse Nationals
1956	Philadelphia Warriors
1957	Boston Celtics
1958	St Louis Hawks
1959	Boston Celtics
1960	Boston Celtics
1961	Boston Celtics
1962	Boston Celtics
1963	Boston Celtics
1964	Boston Celtics
1965	Boston Celtics
1966	Boston Celtics
1967	Philadelphia 76ers
1968	Boston Celtics
1969	Boston Celtics
1970	New York Knicks
1971	Milwaukee Bucks
1972	Los Angeles Lakers
1973	New York Knicks
1974	Boston Celtics
1975	Golden State Warriors
1976	Boston Celtics
1977	Portland Trail Blazers
1978	Washington Bullets
1979	Seattle Supersonics
1980	Los Angeles Lakers
1982	North Carolina
1983	North Carolina State
1983	Philadelphia 76ers

NCAA CHAMPIONS

1939	Oregon
1940	Indiana
1941	Wisconsin
1942	Stanford
1943	Wyoming
1944	Utah
1945	Oklahoma State
1946	Oklahoma State
1947	Holy Cross
1948	Kentucky
1949	Kentucky
1950	CCNY
1951	Kentucky
1952	Kansas
1953	Indiana
1954	La Salle
1955	San Francisco
1956	San Francisco
1957	North Carolina
1958	Kentucky
1959	California
1960	Ohio State
1961	Cincinnati
1962	Cincinnati
1963	Loyola (Illinois)
1964	UCLA
1965	UCLA
1966	Texas El Paso
1967	UCLA
1968	UCLA
1969	UCLA
1970	UCLA
1971	UCLA
1972	UCLA
1973	UCLA
1974	North Carolina State
1975	UCLA
1976	Indiana
1977	Marquette
1978	Kentucky
1979	Michigan State
1980	Louisville
1981	Indiana
1982	North Carolina
1983	North Carolina State

OLYMPIC WINNERS

Date	Venue	Men	Women
1936	Berlin	United States	-
1948	London	United States	-
1952	Helsinki	United States	-
1956	Melbourne	United States	-
1960	Rome	United States	-
1964	Tokio	United States	-
1968	Mexico City	United States	-
1972	Munich	Soviet Union	-
1976	Montreal	United States	Soviet Union
1980	Moscow	Yugoslavia	Soviet Union

WORLD CHAMPIONSHIPS

Date	Venue	Men	Women
1950	Buenos Aires	Argentina	
1953	Santiago	-	United States
1954	Rio de Janeiro	Brazil	-
1957	Rio de Janeiro	-	United States
1959	Santiago	Brazil	-
1959	Moscow	-	Soviet Union
1963	Rio de Janeiro	Brazil	-
1964	Lima	-	Soviet Union
1967	Montevideo	Soviet Union	-
1967	Prague	-	Soviet Union
1970	Lubljiana	Yugoslavia	-
1971	Sao Paulo	-	Soviet Union
1974	Puerto Rico	Soviet Union	-
1975	Bogota	-	Soviet Union
1979	Manila	Yugoslavia	-
1979	Seoul	-	United States
1982	Cali, Colombia	Soviet Union	-
1983	Sao Paulo	-	Soviet Union

COMMONWEALTH CHAMPIONSHIPS

Date	Venue	Men	Women
1978	Coventry	Canada	-
1983	New Zealand	England	Australia

2 Club Directory

MEN'S DIVISION I

BIRMINGHAM

Home Colours Blue and gold.
Home Court Aston Villa Sports and Leisure Centre, 8 Aston Hall Road, Birmingham 6. Tel. 021-328-4884.
Travelling Directions *Road:* The Centre is half-a-mile from Spaghetti Junction – Junction 6 of the M6 Motorway. Take the A38M (City Centre) and leave at the first exit and follow the signs to Aston Villa FC. *British Rail:* Train from Birmingham New Street Station to Aston Station, two minutes walk to the Centre.

BOLTON

Home Colours Yellow with green panels.
Home Court Horwich Leisure Centre, Victoria Road, Horwich, Bolton. Tel. (0204) 692211.
Travelling Directions *Road:* M62 to M61 and follow signs for Preston. Take exit for Horwich and follow to end of dual carriageway. Turn left at roundabout to Horwich centre. At the main traffic lights turn right and then right into Victoria Road.

BRACKNELL

Home Colours Black with gold trim.
Home Court Bracknell Leisure Centre, Bagshot Road, Bracknell, Berks. Tel. (0344) 54203.
Travelling Directions *Road:* North or south on the M3 to junction 3. Follow signs for Bracknell Town Centre. M4 to junction 10 and follow sign posts for Sports Centre. *British Rail:* from Waterloo or Reading to Bracknell.

BRIGHTON

Home Colours Blue.
Home Court The Brighton Centre, Kings Road, Brighton. Tel. (0273) 20313 or Lancing Manor Leisure Centre, Lancing, Sussex. Tel. (09063) 64219.
Travelling Directions LANCING MANOR LEISURE CENTRE *Road:* From north A23 to Robin Hood Garage, follow A27 signposted Worthing. Continue on A27 to Lancing. Centre is on right after Adur Bridge and Shoreham Airport. From west A27 to Lancing. Centre is on left after Lancing roundabout. THE BRIGHTON CENTRE On seafront between Palace Pier and the West Pier.

CRYSTAL PALACE

Home Colours Blue and white.
Home Court Crystal Palace National Sports Centre, Ledrington Road, London SE19. Tel. 01-778 0131.
Travelling Directions *Road:* From north follow A23 or A215 and join A214 to Crystal Palace. Follow signs to National Sports Centre. *Rail:* BR to Crystal Palace from Victoria or London Bridge. The station adjoins the Sports Centre.

DONCASTER

Home Colours Red.
Home Court Concord Sports Centre, Shire Green Lane, Shire Green, Sheffield 5. Tel. (0742) 389274.
Travelling Directions *Road:* Leave M1 at exit 34 (Sheffield/Tinsley). Follow A6109 until signs indicate Wincobank ½ mile City Centre and avoiding 'low bridge'. Turn right and follow road to T junction. Turn right on B6082 and take 3rd left (Newman Road) and at crossroads turn right into Wincobank Avenue. Sports Centre is on the right threequarters of a mile.

HEMEL HEMPSTEAD

Home Colours Orange.
Home Court Dacorum Sports Centre, Park

Road, Hemel Hempstead, Herts. Tel. (0442) 64822/64824.
Travelling Directions *Road:* Leave M1 at exit 8 and follow signs for Hemel Hempstead. At the 4th roundabout take 3rd exit (Kodak building on right). Take first right after Heath Park Hotel (St John's Road) and then 1st right into Park Road. *Rail:* BR to Hemel Hempstead from Euston. Centre is quarter of a mile from station.

KINGSTON

Home Colours Red with blue trim.
Home Court Tolworth Recreation Centre, Fullers Way North, Surbiton, Kingston-upon-Thames, Surrey. Tel. 01-391 0684.
Travelling Directions *Road:* From north or east approach Kingston-upon-Thames from North Circular Road on A307 (via Kew Bridge) or from Central London on A308 (via Putney Bridge). Take A240 from Kingston through Surbiton to Tolworth. At Tolworth underpass turn right onto A3 and at next underpass filter off, turn right round roundabout to take A3 in opposite direction. Take first turning on left (Fullers Way North).
From south enter Tolworth on A240 from Reigate.
From west take A307 from end of M4, or A308 from end of M3 to Kingston.
British Rail: Southern Region to Tolworth from Waterloo.

LEICESTER

Home Colours Blue with yellow and white trim.
Home Court The Granby Halls, Aylestone Road, Leicester. Tel. (0533) 552644.
Travelling Directions *Road:* From north/south exit M1 at junction 21 (A46 to Leicester). At fourth set of lights turn right into Upperton Road (Granby Halls are signposted). At end of Upperton Road, Granby Halls are straight ahead, adjacent to Leicester Tigers RUFC. From Leicester City Centre take signs A50 to Northampton. Granby Halls are on outskirts of Leicester. *British Rail* to Leicester. Granby Halls 10 minutes walk up Waterloo Way.

MANCHESTER

Home Colours Red with black shorts.
Home Court Altrincham Sports Centre, Oakfield Road, Altrincham. Tel. 061-928-2217.
Travelling Directions *Road:* From south leave M6 at junction 19 on to A556. Follow Manchester signs (A56) to Altrincham. Sports centre is in town centre, opposite train and bus stations, over railway bridge. *British Rail* from Manchester Piccadilly to Altrincham. Then as above.

SOLENT

Home Colours Gold with blue trims.
Home Court Fleming Park Sports Centre, Passmore Avenue, Eastleigh, Hants. Tel. (0703) 617416/7.
Travelling Directions *Road:* From north on A33 from Winchester take Eastleigh turn-off. Follow Eastleigh signs and turn right at first set of traffic lights. Sports Centre is on right. *Rail:* To Eastleigh on London-Southampton line. Take Leigh Road opposite station entrance. At first set of traffic lights, turn left into Passmore Avenue. Centre is on right.

SUNDERLAND

Home Colours All blue.
Home Court Crowtree Leisure Centre, Crowtree Road, Sunderland. Tel. (0783) 42511.
Travelling Directions *Road:* Follow A1(M) north and on A690 to Sunderland Centre. Left at the ABC cinema and Centre is 150 metres on the left. *Rail:* BR to Newcastle. By train to Sunderland. Sports Centre is 5 minutes walk through the market square.

WARRINGTON

Home Colours Red with white trim.
Home Court Spectrum Arena, Birchwood, Warrington. Tel. (0925) 817610.
Travelling Directions *Road:* M6 to junction 21 and follow signs for Birchwood. Birchwood Arena approx. 2½ miles from M6 exit. M6 to junction 11 and follow signs to Birchwood.
Note: Car park 4 is closest to the Arena. *Rail:* BR to Birchwood on main Manchester-Liverpool line.

MEN'S DIVISION II

BRADFORD
Home Colours Red with white trim.
Home Court Richard Dunn Sports Centre, Odsal Top, Bradford, West Yorks. Tel. (0274) 307822.

BRUNEL UXBRIDGE
Home Colours Navy with red and white trim.
Home Court Brunel University Sports Centre, Kingston Lane, Uxbridge, Middlesex. Tel. (0895) 52361.

CAMDEN & HAMPSTEAD
Home Colours Gold with black trim.
Home Court Swiss Cottage Baths, Winchester Road, London NW3. Tel. 01-278 4444.

COLCHESTER
Home Colours Gold with navy trim.
Home Court Colchester Sports Centre, Sports Way, Colchester, Essex. Tel. (0206) 64822.

GATESHEAD
Home Colours Blue.
Home Court Gateshead Leisure Centre, Alexandra Road, Gateshead, Tyne and Wear NE8 4JA. Tel. (0632) 773939.

HALIFAX
Home Colours Yellow with red trim.
Home Court North Bridge Leisure Centre, Charlestown Road, North Bridge, Halifax HX3 6TE. Tel. (0422) 41527.

LIVERPOOL
Home Colours Brown and cream.
Home Court Everton Park Sports Centre, Buckingham Street, Liverpool 5. Tel. 051-207-1921.

MANSFIELD
Home Colours Sky blue with maroon shorts.
Home Court Mansfield Leisure Centre, Chesterfield Road South, Mansfield, Nottingham. Tel. (0623) 646081.

NEWCASTLE
Home Colours Black
Home Court Eldon Square Recreation Centre, High Friars, Eldon Square, Newcastle-upon-Tyne NE1 7XY. Tel. (0632) 325917.

PLYMOUTH
Home Colours Yellow with red trim.
Home Court College of St Mark and St John, Derriford Road, Plymouth. Tel. (0752) 777188.

PORTSMOUTH
Home Colours Royal blue, red and white trim.
Home Court Mountbatten Centre, Alexandra Park, Hilsea, Portsmouth. Tel. (0705) 665122.

WATFORD
Home Colours White with blue shorts.
Home Court Watford Leisure Centre, Horseshoe Lane, Garston, Herts. Tel. (09273) 70644.

WEST BROMWICH
Home Colours Green.
Home Court The Gala Baths, Edwards Street, West Bromwich, Sandwell, Midlands. Tel. 021-569-2574.

WOMEN'S DIVISION I

COLCHESTER
Home Colours Navy and gold.
Home Court Colchester Sports Centre, Sports Way, Colchester. Tel. (0206) 64822.

CRYSTAL PALACE
Home Colours Green.
All other details see Division I (Men).

LONDON YMCA
Home Colours Maroon.
Home Court Central London YMCA, 112 Great Russell Street, London WC1B 3NQ. Tel. 01-637 8131.

MANSFIELD
Home Colours Sky blue with maroon shorts.
Home Court Mansfield Leisure Centre, Chesterfield Road South, Mansfield. Tel. (0623) 646081.

NEWCASTLE
See Division II (Men).

NORTHAMPTON
Home Colours Red.
Home Court Lings Forum. The Western Favell Centre, Wellingboro Road, Northampton. Tel. (0604) 402833.

SOLENT
Home Colours Gold and black.
Home Court Redbridge Sports Centre, Cuckmere Lane, Millbrook, Southampton. Tel. (0703) 783330.

SOUTHGATE
Home Colours Green.
Home Court Picketts Lock Sports Centre, Picketts Lock Lane, London N9. Tel. 01-803 4756.

STOCKPORT
Home Colours Red with black trim.
Home Court Peel Moat Sports Centre, Buckingham Road, Heaton Moor, Stockport. Tel. 061-442-6416.

WEST BROMWICH
Home Colours Green.
Home Court The Gala Baths, Edwards Street, West Bromwich, West Midlands. Tel. 021-569-2574.

WOMEN'S DIVISION II

BATH
Home Colours Blue.
Home Court Bath Sports Centre, North Parade, Bath, Avon. Tel. (0225) 62563.

BOLTON
Home Colours White with red shorts.
Home Court Horwich Leisure Centre, Victoria Road, Horwich, Bolton, Lancs. Tel. (0204) 692211.

BRIGHTON
Home Colours Blue.
Home Court Brighton Centre, Kings Road, Brighton, Sussex. Tel. (0273) 20313 or Lancing Manor Leisure Centre, Lancing, Sussex. Tel. (09063) 64219.

DONCASTER
Home Colours Blue and red.
Home Court Adwick Leisure Centre, Welfare Road, Woodlands East, Doncaster, South Yorkshire. Tel. (0302) 721447.

EREWASH
Home Colours Green with yellow trim.
Home Court Sandiacre Friesland Sports Centre, Nursery Avenue. Sandiacre, Derbyshire. Tel. (0602) 296905.

GREAT YARMOUTH
Home Colours Light blue.
Home Court Marina Leisure Centre, Marine Parade, Great Yarmouth. Tel. (0493) 51521.

HEMEL HEMPSTEAD
Home Colours Navy blue with red shorts.
Home Court Dacorum Sports Centre, Park Road, Hemel Hempstead. Tel. (0442) 64822/3.

IPSWICH
Home Colours Green with white trim.
Home Court Northgate Centre, Sidegate Lane, Ipswich. Tel. (0473) 717771.

KINGS LYNN D.F.V.
Home Colours Blue.
Home Court Gaywood Park High School, Sports Hall, Queen Mary Road, Kings Lynn, Norfolk. Tel. (0553) 4671/2.

KINGSTON
See Division I (Men).

LONDON JETS
Home Colours Red with white trim.
Home Court Seymour Hall, Bryanston Place, London W1.

LUTON
Home Colours Wine.
Home Court Stopsley Regional Sports Centre, St Thomas Avenue, Luton, Beds. Tel. (0582) 416772.

SHEFFIELD
Home Colours White.
Home Court Concord Sports Centre, Shiregreen Lane, Shiregreen, Sheffield 5. Tel. (0742) 289274.

SLOUGH
Home Colours Maroon.
Home Court Montem Sports Centre, Montem Lane, Slough. Tel. (0753) 37337.

WANSTEAD GRIFFINS
Home Colours Sky blue with black shorts.
Home Court Wanstead Sports Centre, Red Bridge Lane West, Wanstead, London E11. Tel. 01-989 1172.

JUNIOR DIVISION (MEN)

BIRMINGHAM ATHLETIC INSTITUTE RAINBOW
Home Colours White.
Home Court Birmingham Athletic Institute, John Bright Street, Birmingham 1. Tel. 021-643-5540.

BRACKNELL
Home Colours Blue.
For other information see Division I (Men).

BRADFORD
See Division II (Men).

BRIGHTON
See Division I (Men).

CAMDEN & HAMPSTEAD
See Division II (Men).

CRYSTAL PALACE
See Division I (Men).

COVENTRY
Home Colours Black with red and white trim.
Home Court Coventry Sports Centre, Fairfax Street, Coventry. Tel. (0203) 28601.

EAST LONDON
Home Colours Blue with white trim.
Home Court Morpeth Secondary School, Morpeth Street, London E1.

GATESHEAD
See Division II (Men).

GLOUCESTER
Home Colours White with red shorts.
Home Court Gloucester Leisure Centre, Station Road, Gloucester. Tel. (0452) 36498.

GRAVESEND
Home Colours Green.
Home Court Thong Lane Sports Centre, Thong Lane, Gravesend, Kent. Tel. (0474) 68888.

HALIFAX
Home Colours White.
Home Court See Division II (Men).

HEMEL HEMPSTEAD
Home Colours Orange.
Home Court Dacorum Sports Centre, Hemel Hempstead or St Columbas College, King Henry Lane, St Albans. Tel. (0727) 55185.

KINGSTON
See Division I (Men).

LEICESTER
Home Colours Brown with orange and white trim.
For other information see Division I (Men).

LIVERPOOL
Home Colours Blue with white and red trim.
Home Court Everton Park Sports Centre, Liverpool.
For other information see Division II (Men).

MANCHESTER
See Division I (Men).

MANSFIELD
See Division II (Men).

MILTON KEYNES EAGLES
Home Colours Red and yellow.
For other information see Division II (Men).

NEWCASTLE
See Division II (Men).

PORTSMOUTH
See Division II (Men).

SHEFFIELD
Home Colours Red.
Home Court See Division I (Men).

SUNDERLAND
See Division I (Men).

WARRINGTON
See Division I (Men).

WEST BROMWICH
Home Colours Red.
For other information see Division II (Men).

For other information about basketball contact:

The English Basket Ball Association
Calomax House
Lupton Avenue
Leeds 9
Tel. (0532) 496044/5

Index

A

Abbey Wood, 72
Ackland, Joy, 77, 144
Alcindor, Lew, 127, 131
Aldershot, 32
Alexeeva, Lydia, 68
Amateur Basket Ball Association (ABBA), 30
Ambler, Vic, 30, 50
Anderson, Trevor, 67, 88, 113
Andrew, Carol, 72, 73
Andrezkowski, Kathy, 74
Ashfield Glass, 74
Asia, 134
Assinder, Steve, 54
Athletes in Action, 134
Avenue, 37
Avon Cosmetics, 12, 74
Aztecs, 22

B

backboards, 26
   rules, 39
backdoor, 100
Baillie, Alan, 18
ball, rules, 39
ball handling, 78-97
   dribbling, 78-82
   passing, 82-5
   rebounding, 92-7
   shooting, 85-92
ball out of bounds, rules, 41
Bartanova, Martina, 72
baseball pass, 85
basket, rules, 40
Basketball Association of America, 131
Becker, Tom, 38, 143
behind the back pass, 85
Belk, John, 15
Bell, Cliff, 15
Belov, Alexander, 132, 134
Beswick, Bill, 9, 30, 48, 50, 143
Bett, Mick, 67
Birch, Pauline, 71, 72, 77, 144
Birch, Roy, 68, 71
Birmingham, 27, 149
Birmingham Athletic Institute Rainbow, 153
Black Hills, 131
Bolton, 149, 152
Boorman, Laura, 71, 73
Boston Celtics, 128
bounce pass, 82-5
Brabender, Wayne, 134
Bracknell, 149, 153
Bradford, 151
Bradley, Bill, 134
Brandon, Jimmy, 54, 88, 107
Brazil, 132
Brighton, 149, 152
Broderick, Tom, 54
Brown, Annie, 72
Brunel University, 151
Bruno Roughcutters, 37
Bunting, Allen, 143
Byrd, Alton, 18, 21, 38, 54, 55, 78, 110, 113, 115-18, 122, 143

C

cages, 26
Camden & Hampstead, 151
Camp, Kelly, 74
Central YMCA, 30
centres, 47
Chamberlain, Wilt, 128, 131
Chazalon, Jackie, 72
chest pass, 82-5
China, 134
Cinzano SCP, 38
Clermont Ferrand, 72
coaching, 78-95
Codona, Betty, 77

Codona, Lorraine, 77
Codona, Vanessa, 77
Colchester, 151
Coleman, Brian, 68
Collins, John, 68, 71
Cooper, Bobby, 143
Cooper, Charles, 131
controlled dribble, 80–2
Corbalan, Juan, 78
court, rules, 40
Crystal Palace, 9, 15, 18, 27–30, 32, 37, 38, 110, 149, 151
Crystal Palace Toppies, 74
cup, 35
Curtis, Anita, 72

D

Dalipagic, Dragen, 134
Dassie, Larry, 54, 55
Day, Ian, 15, 54
defensive game, 103–10
    man-to-man defence, 105–7
    zone defence, 108–9
Delibasic, Merza, 134
Detroit Tigers, 11
Donaldson, Dip, 56
Doncaster, 9, 15, 18, 38, 149, 152
dribbling, 78–82
Drollinger, Ralph, 134
dual nationality, 18, 20, 32
Dunn, Bryan, 15
duration, 41

E

Eagles, 72, 77
East London, 153
Embassy All Stars, 30, 37, 38
England, 48–50
England's Women's Team, 68–72
Erewash, 152
European Championship, 145
European Cup, 18, 134
European Cup-winners' Cup, 30, 134

F

fast break, 103, 110
Fédération Internationale de Basketball Amateur (FIBA), 130, 132, 134
Ferris, Candy, 73

foreign players, 32
forwards, 47
fouls, rules, 39, 46–7
    personal, 46
    team, 46–7
    technical, 46
France, 72
free shots, 46, 92
French, Joannie, 73–4

G

Gateshead, 151
give and go, 99
Gloucester, 153
Gollogly, Anne, 71, 72, 77, 144
Gordon, Winston, 67
Gosic, Kresimir, 134
Great Britain's women team, 71
Great Yarmouth, 152
guards, 47
Guymon, Jimmie, 37

H

Halifax, 151
Harkness, Jerry, 131
Harlem Globetrotters, 129, 131
Hartley, Clive, 56
Head, Pat, 68
Hemel Hempstead, 149, 152, 153
Hepp, Ferenc, 71
history of basketball, 22–6
Holylake YMCA, 30
hook pass, 85
hook shot, 92
Hopkins, Neville, 56

I

Innell, Andy, 67
interference, rules, 41
Ipswich, 152
Israel, 71, 134
Istanbul, 48–50
Italy, 134

J

Jabbar, Kareem Abdul, 92, 127–8, 131
Jamestown Community College, 13
Japan, 134
javelin pass, 35

Jeremich, Pete, 15, 18, 32, 85, 110, 122
Johnson, John, 32, 56, 144
Johnson, Magic, 129
Johnson Matthey Trophy, 72
Jones, Jeff, 57
Jones, William, 132
Joseph, Maggie, 74
jump ball, rules, 41
jump shot, 88, 131
Junior Division, 153-4

K

Kings Lynn D.F.V., 152
Kingston, 150
Kirkham, Colin, 67
kit, rules, 40
Kocher, Ken, 57
Korac Cup, 134

L

Last, Joan, 144
Latter Day Saints, 32
lay-up, 88
league championships, 35, 37-8
Legette, Lonnie, 57
Leicester, 27, 150, 153
Lemon, Meadowlark, 129
Lewis, Roy, 67
Liverpool, 151, 153
Lloyd, Dan, 9-21
Lloyd, Dave, 9, 11, 12, 13, 18, 57, 97
Lloyd, Doug, 9, 11, 12, 13, 57
Lloyd, Kathy, 14
London Latvians, 37
London Polytechnic, 30
London YMCA, 151
Loughborough All Stars, 37
Luyk, Clifford, 134
Luton, 152

M

Macauley, Jimmy, 50, 57
Maccabi Tel Aviv, 27
McCray, Greg, 58, 114, 119-22
Mack, Rick, 143
Malone, Moses, 131
Malory, 72
man-to-man defence, 105-7
Manchester, 150

Mansfield, 151
Meneghin, Dino, 134
Mexico, 71
Meyers, Ann, 131
Mikan, George, 88
Millen, Marian, 71
Miller, Debbie, 74
Milton Keynes Eagles, 154
Milwaukee, 127-8, 131
Moore, Joel, 67, 113
Mullins, Pete, 58
Mumford, Kerry, 68
Murray, 18, 38

N

Naismith, James, 22-6, 127, 130, 131
National Basketball Association, (NBA), 126, 131, 134, 147
National Basketball League (NBL), 37-8, 130-1, 143
national championship, 32-5
National College Athletics Association (NCAA), 126
Neal, Curly, 129
netball, 68
New Jersey Nets, 134
New York Knicks, 134
New York Nets, 131
Newcastle, 151, 152
North Carolina State University, 131
Northampton, 152
Nottage, Ken, 58

O

offensive game, 97-103
   backdoor, 100
   fast break, 103
   give and go, 99
   pick and roll, 99-100
officials, 40
Okayama, 134
Olympic Games, 30, 68, 71, 130, 131, 132, 148
O'Shea, Steve, 67
out of bounds, rules, 41
overhead pass, 82, 85
Oxford University, 32

P

Palmer, Danny, 110, 113, 143

passing, 82–5
Pemberton, Ken, 58, 59
Philips tournament, 37
Philip, Paul, 58
pick and roll, 99–100
play, rules, 41
Plymouth, 151
point guards, 47
Poland, 72
Polish Carpathians, 32
Portsmouth, 151
positions, 47

R
RAF Fliers, 37
Real Madrid, 18, 27
rebounding, 92–6
restarting a game, 41
Richards, Paul, 18, 58
Robertson, Oscar, 128
Robinson, T.J., 60, 122
Roma, Bob, 122
Ronchetti Cup, 72
rules, the original, 12
    in detail, 40–7
    summary, 39–40

S
Saiers, Mark, 18, 37, 60, 61, 93, 115, 119, 143
Sailors, Kenn, 131
St Ange, Judy, 72
St Luke's, Exeter, 37
Sampson, Ralph, 128
San Diego, 131
Saperstein, Abe, 129
Saunders, Russ, 21, 60, 62, 115–18, 143
Scantlebury, Peter, 67
Schmitt, Steve, 37
School for Christian Workers, Springfield, 22, 130
scoring, rules, 39, 41
Scottish Women's team, 71
Seattle, 131
Sewell, Drew, 60
Sheffield, 153
Sheffield Hatters, 72
Sheffield YMCA, 37
Shelley, Dave, 60
shooting, 85–92

Shutts, Dave, 78, 110, 122
Slough, 153
Smith, Harry, 38
Solent, 18, 38, 72, 74, 150, 152
South Korea, 71
Southgate, 152
Soviet Union, 68, 132
Spaid, Mike, 60
Spanish Women's team, 71
speed dribble, 80
Springfield College, 22
Sprogis, Peter, 27, 30, 31, 32, 37
Stiller, Sam, 67
Stimpson, Paul, 18, 48, 50, 63, 122–5
Stockport, 9, 15, 74, 152
substitution, 113
Sullivan, Jean, 72
Sunderland, 18, 38, 150
Sutton, 30, 37
Sutton and Crystal Palace, 37

T
Tatham, Karl, 48, 50, 63, 64, 82
Team Fiat, 18, 38
team fouls, 46–7
teams, rules, 39
technical fouls, 46
television coverage, 27
10-second rule, 42
30-second rule, 42
3-second rule, 41–2
through-the-legs pass, 85
Thurston, Kirby, 14
Tieh-chu, Mu, 134
Tigers, 72, 77
time, rules, 39
time-out, 41
Tkachenko, Vladimir, 134
Tober, K., 143
Turkey, 48–50

U
UDT Southgate, 72, 74
United States, 68, 126–31, 132
University College of Los Angeles (UCLA), 127, 128, 131
University of Oregon, 131
Utah Stars, 131

V

violations, rules, 39

W

Wainwright, Jacki, 72, 77, 144
Walton, Kenny, 18, 63
Wanstead Griffins, 153
Warner, Andrea, 144
Warrington, 150
Watford, 151
Watson, Tony, 63
Wearren, Art, 63, 65
West Bromwich, 151, 152, 154
West Germany, 71
Western Carolina University, 13–14
Williams, Earl, 119
Williams, George, 35
Wisman, Tom, 37, 38, 50, 143
Women's basketball, 68–77
Women's European Championships, 68–71
Women's National Cup, 72, 144
Women's National League, 72–7, 144
Women's World Championships, 68
Wordsworth, M., 143
World Championship, 148

Y

Yankton, 141
Yugoslavia, 71, 132, 134

Z

zone defence, 108–10